WINNING CASINO PLAY

ABOUT THE AUTHOR

Avery Cardoza, author of more than 15 books on beating the casino and the world's foremost publisher of games and gambling books, is America's top gambling authority. His definitive book, <u>How to Win at Gambling</u>, the encyclopedic guide to the odds and winning strategies at games of chance, has been called one of the 10 best books on gambling ever written.

Avery Cardoza has counted on his gambling winnings and activities as his primary source of income for all his adult life and before. He has never held a 9-5 job.

No casino will knowingly deal cards to Cardoza, who at the age of 23, when even the biggest casinos refused him play, took his gambling winnings and wrote and published his first book, the best-selling classic, <u>Winning Casino Blackjack for the Non-Counter.</u> Today, with more than 50 gaming titles and 4,000,000 books in print, Cardoza Publishing is the undisputed leader in games and gambling information.

Though originally from New York City, where he is occasionally found, Cardoza has used his winnings to pursue a lifestyle of extensive traveling. Long sojourns to such exotic locales as Bahia in Brazil, Jerusalem, Tokyo and Southeast Asia, were followed by living stints in California, New Orleans, and of course, Las Vegas, where he did extensive research into the mathematical, emotional and psychological aspects of winning.

In 1993, Cardoza also started **Open Road Publishing**, publishing travel guides, and co-authored the <u>Las Vegas Guide</u>. In fall 1994, Cardoza's long-awaited line of winning casino games for the computer will debut.

WINNING CASINO PLAY

Avery Cardoza

Gambling Research Institute
CARDOZA PUBLISHING

to jes

Cardoza Publishing, publisher of Gambling Research Institute (GRI) books, is the foremost gaming and gambling publisher in the world with a library of more than 50 up-to-date and easy-to-read books and strategies.

These authoritative works are written by the top experts in their fields and with more than 4,000,000 books in print, represent the best-selling and most popular gaming books anywhere.

First Edition

Library of Congress Catalog Card Number: 93-74244
ISBN: 0-940685-47-7
Cover photos by Ron Charles

CARDOZA PUBLISHING
P.O. Box 1500, Cooper Station, New York, NY 10276
(718)743-5229

Write for your <u>free</u> catalogue of gambling books, advanced strategies, and computer items.

TABLE OF CONTENTS

INTRODUCTION

You can win money at gambling! Beating the casino at their own game is fun, but is also a skill that must be learned, and in his book we'll show you all the basics needed to gamble intelligently and make you a winner.

We cover the major casino games; blackjack, craps, video poker, slots, and roulette, and show you how to play and win money at each. We also cover the all-important money management skills, skills necessary for a winner to know and use properly.

There's lots of charts and sane advice to help you win, and we go over the winning concepts carefully so that you're fully conversant with the skills necessary to come out ahead while having fun at the tables.

In *blackjack*, you can enjoy a mathematical advantage, and we'll show you how to beat single and multiple deck games; in *craps*, you'll learn how to make the best bets so that the majority of your money goes on wagers the house has no edge on; in *video poker*, we'll show the best machines to play and how to actually have the edge; in *roulette*, how best to play the 150 possible wagers; and in *slots*, how to improve your chances for the big jackpot!

All the winning information you need to get started is here in this book, so read on. Let's beat the casino!

CASINO BASICS

INTRODUCTION

The thrill of gambling, and especially winning, has kept casinos flush with players trying their skills and luck at the games offered. While some players win, and some lose, all players find their hearts beating ever so harder as money laid on the line awaits the laws of almighty chance.

In this section, we'll go over the essentials of playing in a casino - how to deal with changing money and making bets, the currencies used by the casinos, how to get free drinks and cigarettes, what's involved in tipping, and some other basics of the casino setting.

Converting Traveller's Checks and Money Orders to Cash

The dealers accept only cash or chips at the table, so if you bring traveller's checks, money order or the like, you must go to the area of the casino marked **Casino Cashier** to get these converted to cash. Bring proper identification to insure a smooth transaction.

Casino Chips

Chip denominations run in $1, $5, $25, $100 and $500 units. If you're a big stakes player, you may find $1,000, $2,500, $5,000 and $10,000 chips available!

The usual color scheme is as follows: $1 chips are either silver dollars, as in Vegas, or sometimes blue chips, $5 chips - red, $25 - green, and $100 - black.

In casino parlance, $1 chips are called *silver*, $5 chips as *nickels*, $25 chips as *quarters*, and $100 chips as *dollars*. Unless playing at a 25¢ minimum craps table, dollar units are the minimum currency available.

Betting

Casinos prefer that the player uses chips for betting purposes, for the handling of money at the tables, is cumbersome and slows the game. Though bets can be made with cash, all payoffs will be in chips.

House Limits

The house limits will be posted on placards located on each corner of the table. They indicate the minimum bet required and the maximum bet allowed.

Minimum bets range from $1 and $5 per bet, to a maximum of $500, $1000 or $2,000 a bet. Occasionally, 25¢ tables may be found as well, but don't count on it. If special arrangements are made, a player can bet as much as he can muster in certain casinos.

In 1981, a man placed a bet for $777,777 at the Horseshoe Casino in Las Vegas. He bet the don't pass in craps, and walked out two rolls later with one and a half million dollars in cash!

Converting Chips into Cash

Dealers do not convert your chips into cash. Once you've bought your chips at the table, that cash is dropped into a dropbox, and thereafter is unobtainable. When you are ready to convert your chips back to cash, take them to the cashier's cage where the transaction will be done.

Free Drinks and Cigarettes

Casinos offer their customers unlimited free drinking while gambling at the tables or slot machines. In addition to alcoholic beverages, a player can order milk, soft drinks, juices or any other beverages available. These are served by a cocktail waitress.

Cigarettes and cigars are also complimentary and can be ordered through the same cocktail waitress.

Tipping

Tipping, or **toking**, as it is called in casino parlance, is totally at your discretion, and in no way should be considered an obligation.

If you toke, toke only when you're winning, and only if the crew is friendly and helpful to you. Do not toke dealers that you don't like or ones that try to make you feel guilty about not tipping. Dealers that make playing an unpleasant experience for you deserve nothing.

MONEY MANAGEMENT

INTRODUCTION

Winning at gambling requires not only the playing of the correct strategies but also the intelligent use of one's monetary resources. Preparation is key.

To emerge a winner from the streaky swings of fortune inherent in gambling takes a certain degree of emotional control, for the temptation to ride a winning streak too hard in the hopes of a big killing or to bet wildly during a losing streak, trying for a quick comeback, can spell doom.

Big winning sessions can dissipate into small wins or even disastrous losses while moderately bad losing sessions can turn into a nightmare.

Money management is the most important factor in the winning formula, so don't gloss over this section. Without these skills, you cannot win at gambling, even though the odds may favor you. So give this section a good read, and take our advice seriously.

If you do, you'll find yourself on the money end of the table, as a winner, and that's what our goal in gambling is all about!

Money management skills can be divided into the following three categories:

1. Emotional Control

2. Bankrolling (total bankroll, table bankroll)

3. When to Quit (maximize gains, minimize losses).

Before we look at these skills more closely, there's one extremely important point that must be thoroughly understood.

Never gamble with money you cannot afford to lose either financially or emotionally.

Betting with money you cannot afford to lose adversely affects decision making. Rather than playing your best game, your strategy gets restricted to the confines of your monetary or emotional situation, rather than your intelligence and skill.

Betting with "scared money" is a guaranteed way to ensure yourself a losing career as a gambler.

Emotional Control

It is important to recognize that the ups and downs of your moods and feelings affect the quality of your play. A tired player, or an upset player, won't play with a clear head and will make mistakes or unwise decisions that cost money.

But don't let that happen to you. Basically, whenever you feel emotionally unprepared to risk money, it's time to take a break. And if, for whatever reason, the game becomes a cause of anxiety and ceases to be entertainment, than it's time to take a breather.

Play again later on, when you're more alert and

confident. Remember, the casinos aren't going anywhere. There's lots of time to get your bets down.

For gambling to be a pleasurable and successful experience every time you sit down at the tables, you must feel like gambling and must be able to afford possible losses, emotionally as well as financially.

Bottom line, gambling wisely should give you emotional satisfaction, not take it away.

Bankroll Yourself Properly

To be a successful player, your bankroll must be large enough to withstand the normal ups and downs that are the very nature of gambling. Under-capitalization and overbetting are dangerous for two reasons.

First, a normal downward trend can wipe out a limited money supply. Second, and more important, a player feeling pressured by limited capital will play less intelligently than smart play dictates. And that is where you start giving the odds back to the casino and begin playing like a loser.

The key to winning is to play for the win and that means smart money management - using your head. If the amount staked on a bet is over your level, you're playing in the wrong game. Play only at levels of betting you're comfortable with.

Minimizing Losses

Here are three simple guidelines that, if followed, will save you a lot of money.

1. Limit your table losses - Do not dig in for more money, and you can never be a big loser. As they say, the first loss is the cheapest. Take a break, try again later. You never want go get into a position where losing so much in one session totally demoralizes you.

2. Never increase your bets beyond your bankroll range - In other words, always bet within your means.

3. Never increase your bet size to catch up and break even - Raising your bets will not change the odds of the game, nor will it change your luck. What it will do is make your chances of taking a terrible beating frighteningly high. As we discussed earlier do not get into a position where losing so much in one session destroys any reasonable chance of coming out even. You can't win all the time. Rest awhile; you'll get 'em later.

When to Quit - Maximizing Gains

What often separates the winners from the losers is - the winners, when winning, leave the table a winner, and when losing, restrict their losses to affordable amounts. Smart gamblers never allow themselves to get destroyed at the table.

As a player, you have one big advantage that, if used properly, will insure you success as a gambler - You can quit playing whenever you want to. To come out ahead, you must minimize your losses when you lose and maximize your gains when you win. This way, winning sessions will eclipse losing sessions and overall, you'll come out a winner!

Let's move on now to the games themselves!

WINNING AT BLACKJACK

INTRODUCTION

Blackjack turned into the most popular casino game when the word got out - that it can be beaten! With proper play, you can actually have the edge over the casino, and thus, the expectation to win money every time you play!

We cover the fundamentals of casino blackjack here the rules of the game, the players' options, the variations offered in casinos, how to bet, casino jargon, how to play and everything else you'll need to know about playing winning casino blackjack.

BEGINNER'S GUIDE TO CASINO BLACKJACK

Blackjack Table and Layout

Blackjack, or **21** as the game is often called, is played at a curved oval table, with room for five to seven players. The players sit in chairs (or they can stand) around the curved portion of the table, with the dealer on the flat side, standing and facing the players.

On the printed layout, there are corresponding betting spots, usually rectangular, for each participating player. It is here where bets are placed and the cards are dealt. There will also be several of the rules printed on the surface. You'll often see, *Insurace pays 2 to 1, Dealer must draw to 16 and stand on all 17s* and *Blackjack pays 3 to 2.* (See illustration of layout below.) We'll go into these rules in a moment.

The Blackjack Layout

The Decks of Cards

Nevada casinos use one, two, four, six and sometimes as many as eight decks of cards in their blackjack games. Often, within the same casino, single and multiple deck games will be offered.

Typically though, outside of Nevada, multiple deck blackjack dealt out of a shoe is the standard of play in the world whether played in Atlantic City, on casino boats, in Indian casinos or anywhere else blackjack may be found.

When one or two decks are used, the dealer holds the cards in his hand. When more than two decks are used, the cards are dealt from a rectangular plastic or wooden device known as a **shoe**. The shoe is designed to hold multiple decks of cards, and allows the cards to be easily removed one at a time by the dealer.

Each deck used in blackjack is a standard pack of 52 cards, consisting of 4 cards of each value, Ace through King. Suits have no relevance in blackjack. Only the numerical value of the cards count.

Card Values

Each card is counted at face value. 2=2 points, 3=3 points, 10=10 points, while the face cards, Jack, Queen and King, are counted as 10 points. The Ace can be counted as 1 point or 11 points at the player's discretion. When the Ace is counted as 11 points, that hand is called **soft**, as in the hand Ace, 7 = *soft 18*. All other totals, including hands where the Ace counts as 1 point, are called hard, as in the hand 10, 6, A = *hard 17*.

The dealer must count his Ace as 11 if that gives him a hand totaling 17 to 21, otherwise he must count the Ace as 1 point.

In some casinos the rules dictate that the dealer must draw on soft 17. In these casinos, the dealer's Ace will count as 1 point when combined with cards totalling 6 points, and the dealer will have to draw until he forms a hand of at least hard 17.

Casino Personnel

The casino employee responsible for the running of the blackjack game is called the **dealer**. The dealer's duties are to deal the cards to the players, and play out his own hand according to the rules of the game. He converts money into chips for players entering the game or buying in for more chips during the course of the game, makes the correct payoffs for winning hands, and collects bets from the losers.

The dealer's supervisor - technically called the **floorman**, but more commonly referred to as the **pit boss** - is responsible for the supervision of between 4-6 tables. He makes sure the games are run smoothly and he settles any disputes that may arise with a player. More importantly, his job is to oversee the exchange of money and to correct any errors that may occur.

Entering a Game

To enter a blackjack game, sit down at any unoccupied seat at the blackjack table, place the money you wish to gamble with near the betting box in front of you and inform the dealer that you would like to get some chips for your cash. Chips may be purchased in various denominations. Let the dealer know which chips or combination of chips you'd like.

The dealer will take your money and call out the amount he is changing so that the pit boss is aware that a transaction is taking place and can supervise that exchange.

Object of the Game

The player's object in casino blackjack is to beat the dealer. This can be achieved in two ways:

1 - When the player has a higher total than the dealer without exceeding 21.

2 - When the dealer's total exceeds 21 (assuming the player has not exceeded 21 first).

In casino blackjack, as opposed to private games, if the player and the dealer both hold the same total of 21 or less, the hand is a **push**, nobody wins.

Busting or Breaking - Automatic Losers

If the drawing of additional cards to the initial two cards dealt causes the point total to exceed 21, then that hand is said to be **busted**, an automatic loss. Busted hands should be turned up immediately. Once the player has busted, his hand is lost, even if the dealer busts as well afterwards. If the dealer busts, all remaining players automatically win their bets.

Blackjack - Automatic Winner

If the original two card hand contains an Ace with any 10 or face card (J,Q,K), the hand is called a **black-jack**, or **natural**, and is an automatic winner for the player whose bet is paid off at 3 to 2. If the dealer gets a blackjack, all players lose their bets. (The dealer wins only the player's bet, not the 3 to 2 payoff the player receives for a blackjack.)

If both the dealer and the player are dealt a black-jack, the hand is a push. Blackjacks should be turned up immediately.

Payoffs

All bets are paid off at even money ($5 bet wins $5), except in cases where the player receives a blackjack which is a 3 to 2 payoff ($5 bet wins $7.50) or when the player exercises an option that allows him to double his bet. In these instances (doubling and splitting), the payoff is equal to the new doubled bet. If a bet is doubled from $5 to $10, a win would pay off $10.

Single Vs. Multiple Deck Basics

In single and double deck games, the player is dealt his cards face down and gets to physically hold them.

In a game of four or more decks, the cards will be dealt out of a shoe (as opposed to hand-held as in the one or two deck games), and the player is not supposed to touch them at any time. Instead, playing decisions are indicated by hand signals.

Dealer's Rules

The dealer must play by prescribed guidelines. He must draw to any hand 16 or below and stand on any total 17-21. As mentioned above, some casinos require the dealer to draw on soft 17. The dealer has no options and cannot deviate from these rules.

PLAYER'S OPTIONS

Unlike the dealer, the player can vary his strategy. After receiving his first two cards the player has the following options:

Drawing (Hitting)

If the player is not satisfied with his two card total he can draw additional cards. To draw a card, the player scrapes the felt surface with his cards, scraping toward his body. In a game where both the player's cards are dealt face up, the player is not supposed to touch the cards and instead scratches the felt with his index finger or points toward the cards if he desires additional cards.

Single Deck Hitting and Standing

Hitting

Standing

Standing

When a player is satisfied with his original two cards, and doesn't wish to draw additional cards, he signals this by sliding his cards face down under his bet. When the cards are dealt face up, the player indicates his decision to stand by waving his hand palm down over his cards.

Multiple Deck Hitting and Standing

Hitting

Standing

Doubling Down

This option allows the player to double his original bet, in which case he must draw one additional card to his hand and cannot draw any additional cards thereafter. To double down, the player turns his cards face up, and places them in front of his bet. Then he takes an amount equal to his original bet and places those chips next to that bet, so that there are now two equivalent bets side by side.

In games where the cards are dealt face up, the player simply places the additional bet next to his original to indicate the double down.

The dealer will then deal one card face down, usually slipping that card under the player's bet. The bettor may look at that card if he desires.

Splitting Pairs

If dealt a pair of identical value cards, such as 3-3, 7-7, 8-8 (any combination of 10, J, Q, K is considered a pair), the player can split these cards so that two separate hands are formed. To split a pair, the player turns the pair face up, separates them, putting each card in its own place in front of his bet. He then places a bet equal to the original wager behind the second hand. Each hand is played separately, using finger and hand signals to indicate hitting and standing.

Splitting Pairs

Doubling Down

In games where both player cards are dealt face up, the split is indicated by placing the additional bet next to the original one, and after, using hand signals as above to indicate hitting or standing.

If the first card dealt to either split hand has a value identical to the original split cards, that card may be split again (resplit) into a third hand, with the exception of Aces. When the player splits Aces, he can receive only one card on each Ace and may not draw again, no matter what card is drawn.

Doubling Down After Splitting

The player can double down on one or both of the hands resulting from a split according to the normal doubling rules of the casino. This option is offered in all Atlantic City casinos and in certain Nevada casinos.

For example, if a pair of 8s are split, and a 3 is drawn to the first 8 for an 11, the player may elect to double down on that 11. He does so by placing an amount equal to the original bet next to the 11, and receives only one additional card for that hand. The other 8 is played separately and can be doubled as well should an advantageous card such as a 2 or 3 be drawn.

Since options allowed are often in flux, sometimes changing from one month to the next, when playing, check to see if this advantageous option is available.

Surrender (Late Surrender)

The player may "surrender" his original two card hand and forfeit one half of his bet *after* it has been determined that the dealer does not have a blackjack and before the player has exercised any of his other options. Surrender is offered in only a few casinos.

To surrender, the bettor turns and places both his cards face up in front of his bet, and says "surrender," or in a game where both player cards are dealt face up, he announces his intention verbally to the dealer. The dealer will collect the cards and take one half of the bet.

Early Surrender

A player option to give up his hand and lose half his bet *before* the dealer checks for a blackjack. This very favorable option was originally introduced in Atlantic City but is no longer offered because of changes in Atlantic City rules.

Insurance

If the dealer shows an Ace as his upcard, he will ask the players if they want insurance. If any player exercises this option, he is in effect betting that the dealer has a 10-value card as his hole card, a blackjack. To take insurance, the player places up to one-half the amount of his bet in the area marked "insurance."

If the dealer does indeed have a blackjack, he gets paid 2 to 1 on the insurance bet, while losing the original bet. In effect, the transaction is a "standoff," and no money is lost. If the dealer does not have a blackjack, the insurance bet is lost and play continues.

If the player holds a blackjack and takes insurance on the dealer's Ace, the payoff will be even-money whether the dealer has a blackjack or not. Suppose the player has a $10 bet and takes insurance for $5 on his blackjack. If the dealer has a blackjack, the player wins 2 to 1 on his $5 insurance bet and ties with his own blackjack. If the dealer doesn't have a blackjack, the player loses the $5 insurance bet but gets paid 3 to 2 on his blackjack. Either way the bettor wins $10.

Insurance Strategy

Insurance is a bad bet for the following reason:

Making an insurance wager is betting that the dealer has a 10 under his Ace. Since the insurance payoff is 2 to 1, the wager will only be a profitable option for the player when the ratio of 10s to other cards is either equal to or less than 2 to 1.

A full deck has 36 non-tens and 16 tens, a ratio greater than 2 to 1. If the first deal off the top of the deck gives us a hand of 9,7, and the dealer shows an Ace, then we know three cards, all non-tens. Now the ratio is 33 to 16, still greater than 2 to 1, still a poor bet. If you have two 10s for a 20, then the ratio is 35 to 14, making insurance a more costly proposition.

In a multiple deck game, taking insurance is even a worse bet than in a single deck one.

Insuring a Blackjack

Taking insurance when you have a blackjack is also a bad bet, despite the well-intentioned advice of dealers and other players to always "insure" a blackjack. When you have a blackjack, you know three cards, your 10 and Ace, and the dealer's Ace. The already poor starting ratio of 36 tens to 16 non-tens gets worse, becoming 34 to 15 in a single deck game.

Taking insurance when you have a blackjack gives the house an 8% advantage, a poor proposition for the player.

The Play of the Game

The dealer begins by shuffling the cards and offering the cut to one of the players. If refused, it is offered to another player. The dealer then completes the cut, and removes the top card, called the **burn card**. In single and double deck games, the burn card is either put under the deck face up, where all subsequent cards will be placed, or is put face down into a plastic case (procedures vary from casino to casino) to be followed similarly by future discards.

In games dealt out of a shoe, the burn card will be placed most of the way into the shoe and discards will be put in the plastic case.

Players must make their bets before the cards are dealt.

The dealer deals clockwise from his left to his right, one card at a time, until each player and the dealer have received two cards. The players cards are usually dealt face down in a single or double deck game, though it makes no difference if they are dealt face up as they usually are in a game dealt out of a shoe, for the dealer is bound by strict rules from which he cannot deviate.

The dealer deals only one of his two cards face up. This card is called an **upcard**. The face down card is known as the **hole card** or the **downcard**.

If the dealer's upcard is an Ace, he will ask the players if they want insurance. Players that decide to take that option may bet up to one-half their wager in front of their bet in the area marked insurance.

If the dealer has a blackjack, all players that did not take insurance lose their original bets unless a player holds a blackjack also - where it's a push. Players that took insurance break even on the play. If the dealer doesn't have a blackjack, he collects the lost insurance bets and play continues.

Play begins with the bettor on the dealer's left, in the position known as **first base**.

This player has the option to stand, hit, double down, split (if he has two cards of equal value) or surrender (if allowed). A player may draw cards until he is satisfied with his total or busts, or he may exercise one of the other options discussed earlier.

Play then moves to the next player. If any player busts (goes over 21) or receives a blackjack, he must turn over his cards immediately. If a bust, the dealer will collect the lost bet. If a blackjack, the dealer will pay the player 3 to 2 on his bet.

After the last player has acted upon his cards, the dealer will turn his hole card over so that all players can view both of his cards. He must play his hand according to the strict guidelines regulating his play; drawing to 17, then standing. (In some casinos the dealer must draw to a soft 17.) If the dealer busts, all players still in the game for that round of play win automatically.

After playing his hand, the dealer will turn over each player's cards in turn, paying the winners, and collecting from the losers. Once the bettor has played his hand, he shouldn't touch his cards again. He should let the dealer expose his hand which he will do when he has played out his own hand.

In a game dealt from a shoe (four or more decks), the player should never touch the cards anyway.

When the round has been completed, all players must place a new bet before the next deal.

Tipping

The best way to tip a dealer is to place a bet for the

dealer in front of your own bet, so that his chances of winning that toke are tied up with your hand. If the hand is won, you both win together; if the hand is lost, you lose together.

By being partners on the hand, you establish camaraderie with the dealer. Naturally, he or she will be rooting for you to win. This is the best way to tip, for when you win, the dealer wins double - the tip amount you bet plus the winnings from that bet.

RULES AND VARIATIONS
OF THE CASINO CENTERS

Blackjack games are basically the same wherever played, though the rules and variations vary from casino center to casino center, and sometimes, they even differ within a casino itself. However, the strategies we'll show you will arm you for any game, and give you the tools to be a winner no matter the variation.

The standard casino game is the same no matter where you play blackjack.

Following are the main changes you'll find from one game to another, all of them being relatively minor. The first condition favors the player, the second, the house.

• Dealer stands on all 17s vs. dealer hits on soft 17
• Single deck vs. multiple deck (2, 4, 6 or 8 decks)
• Doubling down on any initial two card combination vs. doubling down restricted to certain totals, such as 10 and 11 only.
• Doubling after splitting allowed vs. not allowed

NEVADA RULES

The Las Vegas Strip rules are advantageous to the player and gives one a slight edge on the single deck game if our strategies are followed.

The rule exceptions noted in Downtown Las Vegas and in Northern Nevada games are slightly disadvantageous to the player, but these can easily be overcome by using the winning techniques presented later.

Las Vegas Strip Rules

- Dealer must draw on all totals of 16 or less, and stand on all totals of 17-21.
- Player may take insurance on a dealer's Ace.
- Insurance payoffs are 2 to 1.
- Player receives a 3 to 2 payoff on his blackjack.
- Player may double down on any initial two card combination.
- Identical pairs may be split, resplit, and drawn to as desired with the exception of split Aces, on which the player is allowed only one hit on each Ace.
- One, two, four and bigger deck games are standard.

Downtown Las Vegas Rules

Rules and condition are the same as the Las Vegas Strip rules with one exception:
- Dealer must draw to soft 17.

Northern Nevada Rules

Same as Las Vegas Strip rules with two exceptions:
- Dealer must draw to soft 17.
- Doubling is restricted to two card totals of 10 and 11 only.

Atlantic City Rules

To protect against collusion between the player and the dealer, the dealer does not check his hole card for a blackjack (as is standard in Nevada) until all players have finished playing out their hands.

This safeguard does not affect the player's chances of winning, for if the dealer does indeed have a blackjack, any additional money the player may have wagered on a doubled or split hand will be returned. Only the original bet is lost. The standard rules are:

- Dealer must draw to all totals 16 or less, and stand on all totals of 17-21.
- Player may take insurance on a dealer's Ace.
- Insurance payoffs are 2 to 1.
- Player receives a 3 to 2 payoff on his blackjack.
- Player may double on any initial two card combination.
- Identical pairs may be split but not resplit.
- Doubling after splitting allowed.
- Four, six and eight decks are standard.

European Rules

Blackjack is offered in numerous countries around Europe with the rules and variations changing slightly from place to place. However, the following conditions apply in a good many of these places.

- Dealer must draw to all totals 16 or less, and stand on all totals of 17-21.
- Player may take insurance on a dealer's Ace.
- Insurance payoffs are 2 to 1.
- Player receives a 3 to 2 payoff on his blackjack.
- Doubling Down on 9-11 Only.
- Standees Permitted.
- No Hole Card Rule.
- 4-6 Decks Standard.
- If player draws a 2 on a A8 double down hand, total counts as 11, not 21.

RULES AROUND THE WORLD

Bahamas · Caribbean · Europe ·Southern Africa · Asia · South America · Other Locations

The general blackjack variations we presented under the European Rules are the most prevalent style of play you'll find in casinos around the world. However, you'll find variations from country to country. For example, in Asian and Caribbean casinos, surrender is often allowed. In Great Britain, many European casinos, southern Africa and other locales, you may find doubling after splitting permitted.

In any case, always find out the particular rules of a game before playing so you know what you're up against and how best to play your hands. However, no matter where you play, the game of blackjack is basically the same give or take the minor options discussed, and we'll show you how to win against any variation.

(Note that single deck blackjack is hard to find or nonexistent outside the Nevada casinos. Multiple deck blackjack is the predominant style of play in casinos around the world.)

THE OPTIMAL BASIC STRATEGIES

The Ten Factor

The most striking feature of blackjack is the dominant role that the 10 value cards (10, J, Q, K) play - what we call the **ten factor**.

Collectively, the 10s constitute just under 1/3 of the deck (16 out of 52 cards). Because the 10s are such a dominant factor in a deck of cards, it's correct to think of the dealer's hand as *gravitating* toward a total 10 points greater than his exposed upcard.

Thus, for example, starting out with an upcard of 9, the dealer will make a hand of 19 about 36% of the time and 19 or better 52% of the time.

The Dealer Rules and the Ten Factor

Our strategy is based on the fact that the dealer must play by prescribed guidelines from which he cannot deviate. He must draw to all totals 16 or below, and stand on all totals 17-21 (except in casinos that require the dealer to draw to soft 17). All hard totals that exceed hard 21 are automatic dealer losses.

Our knowledge of the 10 factor and the dealer's rules allows us to separate the dealer's upcards into two distinct groupings: 2s through 6s, the dealer *stiff cards*, and 7s through As (Aces), the dealer *pat cards*.

We'll base our strategies accordingly.

The high concentration of 10 value cards in the deck tells us that the dealer has a good chance of busting when his upcard is a 2, 3, 4, 5 or 6, a *stiff card*, and that there is an excellent chance he will make his hand when showing the *pat cards*, the 7, 8, 9, 10, A. Even when he hasn't a 10 in the hole, combinations such as 89, A7, 99 and so forth, give him an automatic pat hand as well.

General Principles

1. When the dealer shows a 7, 8, 9, 10 or A, hit all hard totals of 16 or below (unless doubling or splitting is more profitable - in any case, you will always draw a card).

2. When the dealer shows a 2, 3, 4, 5 or 6, stand on all hard totals of 12 or more. Do not bust against a dealer stiff card. Exception - Hit 12 vs. 2, 3.

Player Hand of 11 or Less - (Hard Totals)

Always draw to any hard total 11 or less (unless a doubling or splitting option is more profitable). There is no risk of busting, no matter what is drawn, while the drawing of a card can only strengthen our hand.

Player Hand of 17-21 - (Hard Totals)

Always stand on these hard totals (17-21), for the risk of busting is too high to make drawing worthwhile.

Player Hand of 12-16 - (Hard Totals)

With these hands, our play is not an obvious draw such as the 11 or less grouping for the risk of drawing a 10 or other high card and busting is substantial. Our hand is not an obvious stand decision either such as the 17-21 grouping, for the only times we will win with these weak totals of 12-16 are the times that the dealer busts.

It is when we hold hard totals 12-16 (stiffs) that the player's big disadvantage of having to go first (the only built-in house advantage) is a costly proposition. If we draw to hard totals and bust, we are automatic losers. But, on the other hand, if we stand, we will win with these weak totals only when the dealer busts.

It is important to realize that the decision to hit or stand with hard totals 12-16 is a strategy of minimizing losses, for no matter what we do, we have a potentially losing hand against any dealer upcard. Do not expect to win when you hold a stiff.

However, in order to maximize the gain from our overall strategy, we must minimize the losses in disadvantageous situations (as above), and maximize our gains in advantageous ones.

Player Hands 12-16 vs. Dealer Pat Cards 7-Ace

When the dealer's upcard is a 7 through an Ace, you should expect the dealer to make his hand, for he will bust only about one time in four, a mere 25% of the time. If we stand on our hard totals 12-16, we will win only the times that the dealer busts.

You will bust often when drawing to your stiffs, but do not let that dissuade you form hitting your stiffs against pat cards. The strategy on these plays is to minimize losses. We cannot afford to stand and sacrifice our bet to the 3 out of 4 hands that the dealer will make.

When the dealer shows a 7, 8, 9, 10, or Ace, hit all hard totals 16 or below.

Player Hands of 12-16 vs. Dealer Pat Cards 2-6

The greater busting potential of the dealer stiff cards makes standing with hard player totals of 12-16 a big gain over drawing. While we will win only 40% of these hands (the times that the dealer busts), standing is a far superior strategy to drawing, for we will bust too often drawing to our own stiffs against upcards that will bust fairly often themselves.

The times that we would make pat totals by drawing wouldn't guarantee us winners either, for the dealer will often make equal or better totals.

On these plays, our disadvantage of having to go first makes drawing too costly, for once we bust, we automatically lose. Though the dealer will make more hands than bust, our strategy here is to minimize losses so that when we get our good hands, we'll come out an overall winner.

Exception - Hit Player 12 vs. 2, 3

Hitting 12 vs. 2, 3 is the only basic strategy exception to drawing with a stiff total against a dealer's stiff upcard. The double bust factor is not as costly on these plays, for only the 10s will bust our 12. Similarly, the dealer will bust less often showing a 2 or a 3 than with the other stiff cards, 4, 5 and 6.

HITTING AND STANDING - SOFT TOTALS

Player Hand of A2, A3, A4, A5

Unless the player is able to double down, he should always draw a card to these hands. Standing is a poor option, for these totals will win only when the dealer busts. The player has nothing to lose by drawing (no draw can bust these totals), and may improve his total. Players that stand on these hands might just as well give the casinos their money.

Draw on A2-A5 against all dealer upcards.

For soft totals A6 - A9, we want to know:

1- What are our chances of winning by standing?

2- What are the chances of improving our hand by drawing additional cards?

Player Hand of Soft 17 (A6)

Always draw on soft 17 no matter what the dealer shows as an upcard. (In Las Vegas and Atlantic City and other locations where allowed, the correct strategy may be to double down. See doubling section.) This standing total is so weak that attempting to improve our hand by drawing is always a tremendous gain against any upcard.

When a casino requires the dealer to draw to soft

17, it is a disadvantageous rule to the player. Though the dealer will sometimes bust by drawing to a soft 17, in the long run he will make more powerful totals and have more winners. It affects the player the same way.

Player Hand of Soft 18

Against dealer stiff totals of 2, 3, 4, 5 and 6, standing with our 18 is a smart strategy move (unless playing Las Vegas or Atlantic City doubling rules where doubling will often be a big player gain). We have a strong total against these weak dealer upcards.

Stand against dealer upcards of 7 and 8, for our 18 is a solid hand. Against the 7, we have a winning total, and against the 8, we figure to have a potential push, as these dealer upcards gravitate toward 17 and 18 respectively. We do not want to risk our strong position by drawing.

Against the powerful dealer upcards of 9, 10, Ace, our standing total of 18 is a potentially losing hand and thus we try to improve it. Soft 18 is only a fair total and by drawing we are not chancing a powerful total but rather attempting to improve a weak situation.

As a matter of fact, for every 100 plays (at $1 a play) that we draw rather than stand on soft 18 vs. 9 and 10, we will gain $9 and $4 respectively. You must realize that 18 vs. 9, 10, Ace is not a winning hand and since our 18 is a soft total, we have a chance to minimize losses by drawing.

Player Hand of Soft 19 and 20

These hands are strong player totals as they stand. Do not draw any cards. We have no need of improving these already powerful totals.

DOUBLING DOWN

Doubling down is valuable option for it gives the player a chance to double his bet in advantageous situations.

One of the most important factors to consider when contemplating the doubling option is the 10 factor - we are more likely to draw a 10 on our double than any other card value. Thus, doubling on a total of 11, where the drawing of a 10 gives us an unbeatable 21, is a more powerful double than an initial two card total of 9, where the drawing of 10 gives us a strong total of 19, not as powerful as the 21.

On the other hand, we would not double any hand of hard 12 or more, for the drawing of a 10 would bust our total, and we would have an automatic loser at double the bet.

The 10 factor is also an important strategic consideration, for it affects the dealer's busting potential. We double more aggressively against the weakest of the dealer stiff cards, the 4, 5 and 6, and less aggressively against the other stiff cards, the 2 and 3.

The only times we will double against the dealer pat cards are when our doubling totals of 10 and 11, hands that could turn into 20s and 21s, are powerful themselves.

Multiple Deck Doubling Strategy

You'll notice that the doubling strategies for multiple deck play are somewhat less aggressive than the single deck game, a difference we'll discuss later on.

In the following discussion, where multiple deck strategies differ from the single deck, an asterisk will denote the strategy change, and that change will be indicated.

Doubling 11*

This is the strongest doubling hand for the player and should be doubled against all the dealer upcards in a single deck game. If we draw a 10 value card on our double, we will have a 21, the strongest hand we can have. At best, the dealer can tie us.

*Do not double 11 vs. Ace in multiple deck games.

Doubling 10

This is the second strongest doubling hand for the player and should be doubled against the dealer's 2 through 9. Our hard 10 gravitates toward a 20, an overwhelmingly strong hand against these dealer upcards.

Doubling 9*

Double 9 against 2 through 6 only.* The high busting potential of the dealer stiff cards (2-6) makes the 9 a profitable double down. We cannot double down against any of the pat cards (7-Ace) for our win potential when we do draw the 10 (for a total of 19) is not strong enough to compensate for the times when we draw a poor card and cannot draw again.

*Do not double 9 vs. 2 in a multiple deck game.

Doubling 8

Doubling 8 vs. 5, 6 is a valid play in a single deck game only.* Our 8 gravitates toward an 18, only a fair total. However, the very high busting potential of the dealer 5 and 6 make this double a slight gain. Our 8 is not strong enough to make doubling against the other dealer upcards a good play.

*Do not double 8 vs. any upcard in a multiple deck game

DOUBLING DOWN - SOFT TOTALS

The high concentration of 10s play a different role in soft doubling than in hard doubling, for instead of having a positive effect on our chances of making a good total, the drawing of 10 will not even give us a pat hand on many of these doubles.

Doubling with soft totals is generally a gain against weak dealer upcards. The 10 factor figures strongly in the dealer's chances of busting, while on the other hand, the drawing of small and medium cards will often improve our hand to competitive and winning totals.

Doubling A2, A3, A4, A5*

Double A2, A3, A4, and A5 against the dealer's 4, 5, and 6.

The very high busting probabilities of the dealer's 4, 5 and 6 makes doubling with our A2 to A5 profitable for the player. Again, the drawing of a 10 value card does not help our total, but the high dealer busting factor gives us an edge.

We do not double against the 2 and 3, because the dealer will make just too many hands with these upcards. The same is more strikingly true with the dealer pat cards, 7 through Ace.

*Do not double A2 or A3 vs. 4 in a multiple deck game.

Doubling A6*

Double A6 vs. dealer 2, 3, 4, 5, and 6. The A6 is a more powerful double than the A2-A5, for the drawing of a 10 to the A6 will at least give us a pat total and a potential push against a dealer's 17. This "push" factor enables us to gain by doubling against the dealer's 2 and

3 despite the fact that the dealer will make more pat totals than with the weaker upcards 4, 5, and 6.

*Do not double A6 vs. 2 in a multiple deck game.

Doubling A7

Double A7 vs. 3, 4, 5, and 6. Our soft 18 is only a fair total and drawing an additional card won't risk the destruction of a powerful total such as a 19 or 20.

Soft 18 is a strong double against the weaker dealer stiffs 4, 5, and 6, but differs from the soft 17 in that we do not double against the 2. A standing total of 18 vs. a 2 is a stronger winning hand and we do not want to risk the weakening of this hand by doubling and having to draw a card.

Doubling A8, A9

We have two very strong totals here and do not want to risk our excellent chances of winning by attempting to double.

Stand with these powerful hands - do not double.

SPLITTING PAIRS

Splitting can do two valuable things. It can turn one poor total into two stronger hands, such as splitting a hard 16 (8-8) into two hands of 8 each, and it effectively doubles our bet.

The decision to split requires a closer look for we must balance the standing total of our hand against the two proposed split hands, and see if the split and resultant doubling of our bet increases our expectation of winning.

Splitting Pairs - Multiple Deck

You'll notice that we'll split less aggressively against a multiple deck game than against a single deck one. On the other hand, when the game offers doubling after splitting, we get more aggressive.

What happens when a multiple deck game offers doubling after splitting? We'll cover each of the possibilities in turn, showing you the best way to play no matter the situation.

SPLITTING 99

We will examine the decision to split 99 first, for it is a good example of the thinking process involved in splitting. First of all, we should note that this hand totaling 18 is only "fair," not a powerful total like a 19 or 20.

Splitting 9s - Dealer shows a 2, 3, 4, 5, 6

Split 99 against these dealer stiff cards. Our 18 is a winner, but splitting the hand into two halves of 9 each is a big gain. Each starting hand of 9, because of the 10 factor, gravitates toward strong player totals of 19.

The high busting potential of the dealer stiff cards gives us an excellent opportunity to maximize our gain in an advantageous situation.

Splitting 9s - Dealer shows a 7

Stand with 99 vs. dealer 7. We figure the dealer for a 17. Our standing total of 18 is a stronger total and a big potential winner. While splitting 9s will also produce a positive expectation of winning, the risking of our fairly secure 18 against the 7 for two strong but chancy totals reduces the gain.

We have the dealer beat. Stand.

Splitting 9s - Dealer shows an 8

Splitting 99 against the dealer's 8 is a big gain.

Against the dealer's 8, we figure our 18 to be a potential push. However, by splitting the 18 into two separate hands of 9, we hope to turn our possible push into two potential winners. (Each 9 gravitates toward a total of 19, one point higher than the dealer's 18.)

Splitting 9s - Dealer shows a 9

Splitting 99 vs. the dealer's 9 is also a big gain.

Against the 9, our 18 is a losing total, but splitting the 18 into two totals of 9 each reduces our potential loss. Rather than one losing total of 18, we have two potential pushes.

Splitting 9s - Dealer shows a 10 or Ace

Do not split 99 against the dealer's 10 or Ace.

Our split hands of 9 gravitate toward good totals, but against these more powerful dealer upcards, splitting would be a poor play. We do not want to make one loser into two.

Splitting 22 and 33*

Split 22 vs. dealer 3 through 7.*

Split 33 vs. dealer 4 through 7.*

The high busting probabilities of the dealer 4, 5 and 6 makes the 22 and 33 good splits. We split 22 vs. 3 and not 33 vs. 3, because of the lower player busting factor of our split hands of 2 each. The drawing of a 10 gives us another chance to improve on our 2, for correct basic strategy is to draw 12 vs. 3, while the drawing of a 10 on our 3 forces us to stand.

We do not split 22 or 33 vs. the dealer's 2, because

the dealer's 2 does not bust often enough to make splitting a profitable play.

Splitting 22 and 33 vs. 7 seems unusual at first, for this play seems to exceed our normal strategic boundaries of making aggressive plays against the weak dealer stiff cards. Though the 7 is a pat card and will make a lot of pat hands, the 7 will also make the weakest totals, only gravitating toward a total of 17. Our starting totals of 2 and 3 will make hands of 18 or better about one-half the time.

Splitting 22 and 33 against the dealer's 7 will not make us money (because of the high busting factor of our hands), but they will produce a moderate gain over drawing to these hands.

Do not split 22 and 33 against the 8, 9, 10, or Ace. We do not want to make one loser into two losers.

*Multiple deck exception - Do not split 22 vs. 3.

**Games with doubling after splitting allowed (such as Atlantic City) - Split 22 and 33 vs. 2 through 7.

Splitting 44s**

Do not split 44 (unless doubling after splitting is allowed).

The hard total of 8 gravitates toward a total of 18, a far better position than two weak starting totals of 4 each. Against the dealer stiff cards, 2 through 6, we have a big gain by drawing to our 8. While the drawing of 10 will not give us an overwhelmingly strong total, an 18 is far better than drawing the same 10 to a split 4.

We do not want to hold two weak hands of 4 each against the dealer pat cards, especially the dealer's 7 and 8, where we have a good starting total of 8.

**Games with doubling after splitting allowed (such

as Atlantic City) - Split 44 vs. 5 and 6. The added possibilities of being able to double our bet should either or both of the split totals pull well makes this split an advantageous move.

Splitting 55

Never split 55. 55 by itself is an excellent starting total of 10. You do not want to break up this powerful player total into two terrible hands of 5 each. (Our 10 is an excellent doubling hand against dealer upcards of 2 through 9.)

Splitting 66*

Split 66 against dealer stiff cards 2 through 6 only.* Our hard total of 12 is not very favorable, nor are the split hands of 6 and 6 too promising either. We have a losing hand either way against all dealer upcards. However, we want to minimize our losses.

Against the dealer stiff cards 2, 3, 4, 5, and 6, our split hands of 6 and 6 will sometimes draw cards to give us pat totals of 17-21.

Of course, we will often end up with stiff totals on the split pair (by the drawing of a 10 or other sufficiently large card) and be forced to stand. But the high dealer busting factor makes splitting 66 against the dealer stiffs a slight gain.

Obviously we will not split 66 against the dealer pat cards. We don't need two hands of 16 against a card that will bust only one time in four.

*Multiple deck exception - Do not split 66 vs. 2.

**Games with doubling after splitting allowed (such as Atlantic- City) - no exceptions. Split 66 vs. 2-6.

Splitting 77

Split 77 against dealer upcards of 2, 3, 4, 5, 6, and 7. Against the dealer stiff cards 2 through 6, two playable hands of 7 and 7 are preferable to one stiff total of 14. Splitting 77 is not a strong split, for these totals only gravitate toward a 17, but the high busting rate of the dealer stiff cards makes this split a big gain.

Splitting 77 against the dealer's 7 is also an excellent split, for we are taking one losing total of 14 into two potential pushes of 17 each.

We don't split 77 vs. the dealer's 8, 9, 10, and Ace. We do not want to take one poor total of 14 into two hands gravitating toward a second best total of only 17.

Splitting 88

Split 88 against all dealer upcards. Against the dealer's 2 through 8, we are taking one terrible hand of 16 into two playable totals of 8 each. There is a tremendous gain on all these plays.

Splitting 88 against the dealer's 9, 10, A are the strangest of the basic strategy plays. While splitting this 16 into two hands of 8 and 8 is not a winning situation against the strong dealer upcards of 9, 10, and A, it is an improvement over our very weak total of hard 16.

Bear with this unusual play, for computer simulation studies have played out the hand millions of times for both drawing and splitting, and found that the player loses less by splitting 88. Although this split is weak, it produces a gain over drawing to the easily bustable 16.

Splitting 10, 10

Do not split 10s. The hard total of 20 is a winning hand against all dealer upcards. Splitting 10s against any dealer upcard is a terrible play, for you are taking one "solid" winning hand into two good but uncertain wins.

Splitting AA

Split AA against all dealer upcards. Each Ace is a powerful starting total of 11 points. If we draw the 10, our 21 can't be beat. Splitting AA is a tremendous gain against all dealer upcards.

HOW TO USE THE STRATEGY CHARTS

In all our charts on the following pages, the dealer's upcard is indicated by the horizontal number (running left to right) on the top row, and the player's hand is indicted by the vertical numbers (up and down) in the left column. The letters in the matrix indicate the correct strategy play.

For example, in the following chart, if you're dealt an A6 and the dealer shows a 7 as an upcard, the "H" in the matrix shows that hitting is the correct play.

Strategy when Doubling Down is Restricted

In Northern Nevada and other locations where doubling is restricted, usually to 10 and 11, hit instead of doubling down on all hands where "D" is indicated, except on A7, where you should stand.

SINGLE DECK MASTER CHART

	2	3	4	5	6	7	8	9	10	A
7/less	H	H	H	H	H	H	H	H	H	H
62	H	H	H	H	H	H	H	H	H	H
44/53	H	H	H	D	D	H	H	H	H	H
9	D	D	D	D	D	H	H	H	H	H
10	D	D	D	D	D	D	D	D	H	H
11	D	D	D	D	D	D	D	D	D	D
12	H	H	S	S	S	H	H	H	H	H
13	S	S	S	S	S	H	H	H	H	H
14	S	S	S	S	S	H	H	H	H	H
15	S	S	S	S	S	H	H	H	H	H
16	S	S	S	S	S	H	H	H	H	H
A2	H	H	D	D	D	H	H	H	H	H
A3	H	H	D	D	D	H	H	H	H	H
A4	H	H	D	D	D	H	H	H	H	H
A5	H	H	D	D	D	H	H	H	H	H
A6	D	D	D	D	D	H	H	H	H	H
A7	S	D	D	D	D	S	S	H	H	H
A8	S	S	S	S	S	S	S	S	S	S
A9	S	S	S	S	S	S	S	S	S	S
22	H	spl	spl	spl	spl	spl	H	H	H	H
33	H	H	spl	spl	spl	spl	H	H	H	H
44	H	H	H	D	D	H	H	H	H	H
55	D	D	D	D	D	D	D	D	H	H
66	spl	spl	spl	spl	spl	H	H	H	H	H
77	spl	spl	spl	spl	spl	spl	H	H	H	H
88	spl	spl	spl	spl	spl	spl	spl	spl	spl	spl
99	spl	spl	spl	spl	spl	S	spl	spl	S	S
10/10	S	S	S	S	S	S	S	S	S	S
AA	spl	spl	spl	spl	spl	spl	spl	spl	spl	spl

S = Stand   H = Hit   D = Double   Spl = Split

47

MULTIPLE DECK MASTER CHART

	2	3	4	5	6	7	8	9	10	A
7/less	H	H	H	H	H	H	H	H	H	H
62	H	H	H	H	H	H	H	H	H	H
44/53	H	H	H	H	H	H	H	H	H	H
9	H	D	D	D	D	H	H	H	H	H
10	D	D	D	D	D	D	D	D	H	H
11	D	D	D	D	D	D	D	D	D	H
12	H	H	S	S	S	H	H	H	H	H
13	S	S	S	S	S	H	H	H	H	H
14	S	S	S	S	S	H	H	H	H	H
15	S	S	S	S	S	H	H	H	H	H
16	S	S	S	S	S	H	H	H	H	H
A2	H	H	H	D	D	H	H	H	H	H
A3	H	H	H	D	D	H	H	H	H	H
A4	H	H	D	D	D	H	H	H	H	H
A5	H	H	D	D	D	H	H	H	H	H
A6	H	D	D	D	D	H	H	H	H	H
A7	S	D	D	D	D	S	S	H	H	H
A8	S	S	S	S	S	S	S	S	S	S
A9	S	S	S	S	S	S	S	S	S	S
22	H	H	spl	spl	spl	spl	H	H	H	H
33	H	H	spl	spl	spl	spl	H	H	H	H
44	H	H	H	H	H	H	H	H	H	H
55	D	D	D	D	D	D	D	D	H	H
66	H	spl	spl	spl	spl	H	H	H	H	H
77	spl	spl	spl	spl	spl	spl	H	H	H	H
88	spl	spl	spl	spl	spl	spl	spl	spl	spl	spl
99	spl	spl	spl	spl	spl	S	spl	spl	S	S
10/10	S	S	S	S	S	S	S	S	S	S
AA	spl	spl	spl	spl	spl	spl	spl	spl	spl	spl

S = Stand   H = Hit   D = Double   Spl = Split

48

ATLANTIC CITY MULTIPLE DECK MASTER CHART

	2	3	4	5	6	7	8	9	10	A
7/less	H	H	H	H	H	H	H	H	H	H
8	H	H	H	H	H	H	H	H	H	H
9	H	D	D	D	D	H	H	H	H	H
10	D	D	D	D	D	D	D	D	H	H
11	D	D	D	D	D	D	D	D	D	H
12	H	H	S	S	S	H	H	H	H	H
13	S	S	S	S	S	H	H	H	H	H
14	S	S	S	S	S	H	H	H	H	H
15	S	S	S	S	S	H	H	H	H	H
16	S	S	S	S	S	H	H	H	H	H
A2	H	H	H	D	D	H	H	H	H	H
A3	H	H	H	D	D	H	H	H	H	H
A4	H	H	D	D	D	H	H	H	H	H
A5	H	H	D	D	D	H	H	H	H	H
A6	H	D	D	D	D	H	H	H	H	H
A7	S	D	D	D	D	S	S	H	H	H
A8	S	S	S	S	S	S	S	S	S	S
A9	S	S	S	S	S	S	S	S	S	S
22	spl	spl	spl	spl	spl	spl	H	H	H	H
33	spl	spl	spl	spl	spl	spl	H	H	H	H
44	H	H	H	spl	spl	H	H	H	H	H
55	D	D	D	D	D	D	D	D	H	H
66	spl	spl	spl	spl	spl	H	H	H	H	H
77	spl	spl	spl	spl	spl	spl	H	H	H	H
88	spl	spl	spl	spl	spl	spl	spl	spl	spl	spl
99	spl	spl	spl	spl	spl	S	spl	spl	S	S
10/10	S	S	S	S	S	S	S	S	S	S
AA	spl	spl	spl	spl	spl	spl	spl	spl	spl	spl

S = Stand   H = Hit   D = Double   Spl = Split

EUROPEAN STYLE MULTIPLE DECK MASTER CHART

	2	3	4	5	6	7	8	9	10	A
7/less	H	H	H	H	H	H	H	H	H	H
8	H	H	H	H	H	H	H	H	H	H
9	H	D	D	D	D	H	H	H	H	H
10	D	D	D	D	D	D	D	D	H	H
11	D	D	D	D	D	D	D	D	H	H
12	H	H	S	S	S	H	H	H	H	H
13	S	S	S	S	S	H	H	H	H	H
14	S	S	S	S	S	H	H	H	H	H
15	S	S	S	S	S	H	H	H	H	H
16	S	S	S	S	S	H	H	H	H	H
A2	H	H	H	D	D	H	H	H	H	H
A3	H	H	H	D	D	H	H	H	H	H
A4	H	H	D	D	D	H	H	H	H	H
A5	H	H	D	D	D	H	H	H	H	H
A6	H	D	D	D	D	H	H	H	H	H
A7	S	D	D	D	D	S	S	H	H	H
A8	S	S	S	S	S	S	S	S	S	S
A9	S	S	S	S	S	S	S	S	S	S
22	H	H	spl	spl	spl	spl	H	H	H	H
33	H	H	spl	spl	spl	spl	H	H	H	H
44	H	H	H	H	H	H	H	H	H	H
55	D	D	D	D	D	D	D	D	H	H
66	spl	spl	spl	spl	spl	H	H	H	H	H
77	spl	spl	spl	spl	spl	spl	H	H	H	H
88	spl	spl	spl	spl	spl	spl	spl	spl	spl	spl
99	spl	spl	spl	spl	spl	S	spl	spl	S	S
XX	S	S	S	S	S	S	S	S	S	S
AA	spl	spl	spl	spl	spl	spl	spl	spl	spl	spl

S = Stand   H = Hit   D = Double   Spl = Split

Single & Multiple Deck Differences

The greater number of cards used in a multiple deck game makes the removal of any particular card or cards less significant compared to a single deck game, and as a result, our doubling and splitting strategies are less aggressive.

For example, the removal of three cards (5,3,5) creates a favorable imbalance for the player in a single deck game and makes a 53 double vs. the dealer's 5 a profitable play. The effective removal of these three cards gives the player a better chance of drawing a 10 on his 8 and, at the same time, increases the dealer's chance of busting. In a single deck game, 53 vs. 6 is a favorable double.

However, the removal of these three cards are barely felt in a multiple deck game, and thus, no favorable imbalance has been created and the double down is not a correct play. This lack of sensitivity to particular card removal in multiple deck games accounts for the following nine changes in the doubling and splitting strategies.

Otherwise, multiple deck basic strategy is identical to the single deck basic strategy.

In a multiple deck game:
- 1- Do not double hard 8 vs. 5; hit instead.
- 2- Do not double hard 8 vs. 6; hit instead.
- 3- Do not double hard 9 vs. 2; hit instead.
- 4- Do not double hard 11 vs. Ace; hit instead.
- 5- Do not double A2 vs 4; hit instead.
- 6- Do not double A3 vs. 4; hit instead.
- 7- Do not double A6 vs 2; hit instead.
- 8- Do not split 22 vs. 3; hit instead.
- 9- Do not split 66 vs. 2; hit instead.

PLAYER'S OPTIONS

Use these strategies where the following options are permitted:

Doubling Down Permitted After Splitting

A standard option in Atlantic City, but offered only in a few Nevada casinos. It allows you to double down on one or more of the hands resulting from a split according to the standard doubling rules of the casino.

When this option is permitted, you'll split more aggressively to take advantage of good doubling situations that can arise as a consequence of the split.

This option is favorable to the player.

Our Hand		Single Deck	Multiple Deck
22	split against	2-7	2-7
33	split against	2-7	2-7
44	split against	4-6	5-6
66	split against	2-7	2-6
77	split against	2-8	2-7

Late Surrender (Surrender)

A player option to forfeit his hand and lose half his bet after it has been determined that the dealer does not have a blackjack. This option is favorable to the player.

Our Hand		Single Deck	Multiple Deck
16*	surrender against	10, A	9, 10, A
15	surrender against	10	10
77	surrender against	10	

*Split 88 - Do not surrender

Early Surrender

A player option to forfeit his hand and lose half his bet *before* the dealer checks for a blackjack. A rare option, but extremely valuable for the player if available.

Dealer's Upcard		Player's Totals
A	early surrender with	5-7, 12-17
10	early surrender with	14-16
9	early surrender with	16*

Do not surrender soft totals

*Split 88 - Do not early surrender

WINNING STRATEGIES

By following the basics strategies we showed earlier, you're already starting with an even or near even game.* That already makes you better than 95% of the players who play the game.

To get an actual mathematical advantage over the casino and the expectation to win money every time you play, requires the use of professional card counting or non-counting techniques.

While these professional strategies are beyond the scope of this work, (see ads in the back for professional level strategies) we'll show you a few basic principles to increase the strength of your game.

First, we must understand the nature of blackjack and we'll begin with the cards themselves and how they relate to your chances of winning.

*If you play perfect basic strategy as we've shown, and the game is a single deck game with the favorable Las Vegas Strip rules, the game is dead-even - the house has no edge on you! If the particular game has less liberal rules (Northern Nevada) or is a multiple deck game, the house enjoys a slight initial edge.

The Value of the Cards

Tens and Aces are the most valuable cards for the player. When there is a higher ratio of these cards in the deck than normal, the odds shift in the player's favor. Conversely, when there is a smaller ratio of these high cards in the deck, meaning there are more smaller cards (2 through 7) than normal, cards that favor the house, the odds shift in the casino's favor. The 8s and 9s are relatively neutral.

You can achieve an extra edge in blackjack by playing an "eyeballing strategy." When a lot of tens and aces seem to have been already played, more than the normal amount, you bet less. The aces and tens are cards you need in the deck. On the other hand, when a lot of small cards (more than normal) have been played, than you bet more. The valuable tens and Aces remain in abundance and thus you are in a favorable situation.

Every time the deck is shuffled, start your estimation of tens and aces over again. We're tracking cards dealt from a depleted deck of cards. Once the deck has been shuffled, the game is fresh and we must begin fresh.

This simple strategy is most effective in single deck blackjack, and less so, incrementally, in two, four, six and eight deck games where the overall number of the cards is less susceptible to composition changes from just a few cards being removed.

Obviously, you cannot win as much without using professional card counting or non-counting techniques, but combining the eyeballing strategy with the basic strategies we've presented gives you a very strong game against any casino.

Bet Range

I recommend a bet range of 1-4 units. Thus, if $5 is your standard bet, your maximum bet should not exceed $20. Similarly, $10 bettors should hold their maximum bets at $40, $25 bettors to $100, and $100 bettors to $400.

The ranging of your bets from one unit in disadvantageous situations to four units in highly advantageous situations is a wide enough bet spread to maximize your gains while at the same time minimizing your risk.

Becoming a Better Blackjack Player

If you're a serious player and want to really get the edge over the casino and be a consistent winner at blackjack, you'll want to learn either a counting system or the advanced non-counter strategy. However, before anything else, you must learn the optimal basic strategies in this book if you want to be a winner. All advanced strategies assume this knoweldge.

Here's the two choices you have for becoming a better player.

Choice number one is that you can purchase the simple-to-use Cardoza Non-Counter Multiple Deck Strategy. This will give you an edge of about 1/2 - 1%. This brand new strategy was developed for players who are intimidated by counting cards and it actually allows non-counting players the mathematical edge over the casino in multiple deck games. This strategy is our own research and is brand new.

The second choice is the Cardoza Base Count Strategy, or even better, the home instruction course, (which includes the Base Count Strategy) designed for serious players who want to work just a little harder.

These card counting strategies give you an edge of from 1-3% over the casino and put you on a professional level of play. You'll learn advanced betting and playing strategies and receive full strategy charts that will prepare you for every situation. No longer will those 15s and 16s be busted with big bets on the table!

These card counting strategies and the exciting new Multiple Deck Non-Counter can be ordered through the coupons in the back of the book.

Winning Summary

We've covered a lot of ground in this section, showing you how to play your hands and how to optimally use all the options available at blackjack. A lot of money can be made at blackjack, which is why the game is so popular, but as you see, you must invest a little time in learning how to play the game properly.

Blackjack is a percentage game that can be beat, but to win, you've got to stick by your guns, and always make the correct percentage plays as we've showed you here. Thse strategies are computer-proven and 100% accurate. You won't win every hand, nor will you win every session. However, with correct play, you can be an overall winner at blackjack.

Good Skill!

WINNING
AT
CRAPS

INTRODUCTION

Craps is the most exciting of the casino games, for the action is fast, and a player catching a good roll can win large sums of money quickly. But big money can be lost just as fast unless the player is conversant with the best bets available and knows how to use them in a coordinated strategy.

We'll go over the fundamentals of playing casino craps in this section, and not only explain all the bets available and show you which wagers are the best to make, but also, we'll show you how to play these bets so that when the smoke clears, you'll have the best chances of emerging a winner.

Let's get on with it, and let the dice roll!

BEGINNER'S GUIDE TO CASINO CRAPS

The Table

The standard casino craps table is oval in shape and depending upon the particular size is built to accommodate between 15 to 24 players.

The sides of the table are several feet above the layout where the bets are made, giving the players an edge to lean on, and giving the dice walls to carom off.

The Layout

The craps layout is divided into three distinct sections. The two end sections, which are identical, are areas around which the players cluster, and where the majority of bets are made. Each end area is run by one of the standing dealers.

The middle area is flanked on either side by a boxman and stickman. This area contains the proposition, or center bets, and is completely under the jurisdiction of the stickman.

The layout is a large piece of green felt with various imprints marking the plethora of bets possible. All action is centered on the layout. Bets are placed, paid off and collected on this felt surface. And, of course, it is on the layout where the dice are thrown.

Layouts around the world are basically the same, though some clubs may have slight variations, but none of these need concern us, for the game of craps is similar whatever casino you play in. The minor variations that do occur, concern bets whose odds are so poor that we wouldn't want to make them anyway.

The following page shows a standard craps layout.

Craps Layout

The Dice

The game of craps is played with two standard six-sided dice, with each die numbered from 1 to 6. The dice are manufactured so that they fall as randomly as possible, with a 5 being just as likely to fall on one die as a 3. However, we'll see later that combining two dice together creates some combinations that are more likely to appear than others, and this is the basis of the odds in craps.

Players

Only one player is needed to play craps, while as many as can fit around a craps table are the maximum. When the action is hot and heavy, bettors will be lined up shoulder to shoulder, screaming, yelling and cajoling, for the dice to come through and make them winners.

CASINO PERSONNEL

The average craps table is manned by a crew of four casino employees - one **stickman**, who stands at the center of the table, two **dealers**, who stand on the opposite side of the stickman at either end of the table, and a **boxman** who is seated between the two standing dealers and directly across from the stickman.

Let's look at the function of each crewman in turn.

The Stickman

The **stickman's** main responsibility is the handling of the dice, a task he performs with a flexible, hooked stick. When a new shooter is coming-out, the stickman will offer him a cache of dice to choose from, and after two have been selected, will return the remaining dice to his box.

After each roll of the dice, the stickman will announce the number thrown and bring the dice back to the center of the table. Usually, he will supply additional information about its consequences.

If a 7 is thrown on the come-out roll, he may announce, "7, winner on the pass line."

If instead, a 2, 3 or 12 is rolled on the come-out, he may say, "Craps, line away." When a shooter sevens-out, the stickman might exclaim, "7 out, line away."

A good stickman is a show in himself, and by the excitement he generates, makes the game more lively and colorful for both the players and the dealers. And from the casino's standpoint, happy players tend to bet heavier and wilder than they normally would.

The dice will be returned to the shooter after the dealers have finished making payoffs.

The stickman is also responsible for the proposition, or center bets made in the middle of the layout. He will place all proposition bets directed his way into their proper location on the layout.

If these bets are winners, the stickman will direct the dealers to pay off the winning players, and if the bets are losers, he will collect the lost bets and push them over to the boxman.

The Dealers

There is a dealer located on either side of the boxman, and his main responsibility is the handling of all the monetary transactions and betting on his end of the table. He pays off winning bets and collects losing ones, converts cash into chips, and will change chips into higher or lower denominations for the player.

Though the player can make many of the bets himself, there are wagers such as the place bets and certain free-odds bets which must be given to the dealer to be placed.

Each standing dealer has a **marker buck**, a plastic disk used to indicate the established point. If a player is coming-out, beginning his roll, the marker buck will be lying on its black side, labeled "**off**," and if a point is established, the dealer will flip the marker buck to the white side, marked "**on**," and place it in the appropriately numbered box to indicate the point.

It is with the dealers that the player will have most of his contact and to whom he can address his questions.

The Boxman

The **boxman** sits between the two dealers and across from the stickman, and from this central position, supervises the running of the craps table. His job is not only to watch over the casinos bankroll, most of which sits right in front of him in huge stacks, but to make sure the dealers make the correct payoffs so that neither the player nor the house gets shorted.

He is responsible for settling any disputes that may arise between the players and the dealers. Generally, the benefit of the doubt will be given to the player on any disputed call. If the dice leave the table for any reason, the returned dice are brought directly to the boxman for inspection. He'll check the logo and coded numbers on the dice to make sure they haven't been switched, and will inspect the surfaces for imperfections that may influence the game. If, for any reason, the boxman feels suspicious of the returned dice, he'll remove them from play and have the stickman offer the shooter a new pair.

When one boxman is on duty, he will supervise one end of the table while the stickman watches the other.

However, when the action is fast, and stacks of chips are riding on each roll of the dice, a second boxman will often be added to the crew to help watch the table. In these cases, the boxmen will sit next to each other behind the chips, each being responsible for one end of the table.

In addition to the boxmen, there are other supervisors, called floormen and pit bosses, who watch over the action from behind the boxman in the area known as the pit.

The Pit

Craps tables are arranged in a pattern so that a central area, known as the **pit**, is formed in the middle. The tables are arranged around the pit so that the boxmen and standing dealers have their backs to the pit area, and so that the floormen, standing inside the pit, can easily watch over all of the craps tables.

Floormen

The **floormen** spend their entire shift on their feet, and are responsible for supervising a particular table or group of tables in the pit.

In addition to these supervisory capacities, they deal with players that have established credit lines. If a player requests credit, the floorman checks to see if his credit is good, and if verified, authorizes the dealer to give the requested chips. At the same time, or soon afterwards, he will bring the player an IOU to sign, acknowledging the credit transaction.

The Pit Boss

The **pit boss**, under whose authority the floormen work, is in charge of the entire craps pit. He's rarely in contact with the players, unless a high roller is playing, whereby he may come over and introduce himself or offer the roller some **comps** (freebies).

Entering a Game

To enter a craps game, slip into a space by the rail of the craps table. After catching the dealer's attention, place your cash on the layout and inform him of the denomination of chips you would like. The dealer will take your money, and give it to the boxman who will supervise the exchange.

Tipping

Tips are shared by the crew working the craps table. Though the usual tip is to make a proposition bet, with the exclamation "one for the boys," a better way to toke the crew would be to make a line bet for them, so they can have a good chance of winning the bet.

Dealers prefer this type of tip for they too are aware how poor the proposition bets are. This is also better than just handing over the toke, for if the bet is won, the dealer wins double for the tip - the amount bet for him plus the winnings from that bet.

Play of the Game

When a new player is to throw the dice, the stickman will empty his box of dice and push them across the layout with his stick. After this player, known as the **shooter**, selects two dice of his choice, the stickman will retrieve the remaining dice and return them to his box.

In a new game, the player closest to the boxman's left side will receive the dice first, and the rotation of the dice will go clockwise from player to player around the craps table.

The shooter has no advantage over the other players except perhaps the psychological edge he may get throwing the dice himself. He is required to make either a pass or don't pass bet as the shooter, and in addition, can make any other bets allowed.

There are a wide variety of bets the players can make, and these bets should be placed before the shooter throws the dice. Players can bet with the dice or against them at their preference, but in either case, the casino will book all wagers.

The shooter is supposed to throw the dice so that they bounce off the far wall of the table. If the throw does not reach the far wall, the shooter will be requested to toss harder on his next throw, and if he persists in underthrowing the dice, the boxman may disallow him from throwing further.

This policy protects against cheats that can manipulate unobstructed throws of the dice.

The Come-Out Roll

The first throw of a shoot is called the **come-out roll**. It is either an automatic winner or loser for players betting with the dice, called **right bettors**, or those betting against the dice, called **wrong bettors**; or the come-out roll can establish a point which the shooter hopes to repeat before a 7 is thrown.

The come-out roll works as follows. The throw of a 7 or 11 on the come-out roll is an automatic winner for the pass line bettors, players betting that the dice will win, or pass, while the throw of a **craps**, a 2, 3 or 12 is an automatic loser.

For the don't pass bettors, those betting against the dice, the come-out roll works almost exactly opposite to the pass line bet. A come-out roll of a 7 or an 11 is an automatic loser, a 2 or a 3 an automatic winner, while the 12 (in some casinos a 2 instead) is a standoff.

If the come-out roll is an automatic decision, a 2, 3, 7, 11 or 12, the affected players will have their bets paid or collected, and the following roll will be a new come-out roll.

Any other number thrown, a 4, 5, 6, 8, 9 or 10, becomes the **point**, and the dealers will indicate this by flipping their respective marker bucks to the white side marked "on," and move the disk into the rectangular numbered boxes corresponding to the point number thrown.

Once a point is established, only the 7 and the point are consequential rolls for the pass and don't pass bettors, also called **line bettors**. All other rolls are neutral throws for these bets.

The shoot will continue until either the point is repeated, a winner for the pass line bettors and a loser for the don't pass bettors, or until a seven is thrown, known as **sevening-out**, a loser on the pass line and winner on the don't pass. In either case, the shoot will have been completed, and the following roll will be a new come-out roll, the start of a new shoot.

There are many other bets available to the player as we will discuss later, some that can be made only after a point is established, and others that can be made at any time during a shoot. So while the line bettors may not be affected by a particular throw, the dealers may be paying off or collecting chips on other affected wagers while the shoot is in progress.

The shooter can continue throwing the dice until he sevens-out. Then, after all affected bets are settled on the layout, the stickman will present his collection of dice to the next player in a clockwise rotation. Even though the shooter may **crap-out** (the throw of a 2, 3 or 12) on his come-out roll, a losing roll for the pass line bettors, the shooter does not have to yield the dice.

It is only when the shotter throws a 7 before his point repeats, *sevens-out*, that the dice must be relinquished.

The Come-Out Roll Capsulated

The come-out roll occurs when:
1 - A new shooter takes the dice.
2 - The shooter throws a 2, 3, 7, 11 or 12 on the come-out roll, an automatic winner or loser for the line bettors.
3 - After a point is established, the shooter either repeats that point or sevens-out.

Betting Right or Wrong

Betting right or wrong are only casino terms used to designate whether a player is betting with the dice, **betting right**, or betting against the dice, **betting wrong**, and are in no way indicative of a correct or incorrect way of playing. As we shall see, both ways of betting are equally valid.

UNDERSTANDING THE ODDS

Craps is played with two dice, individually called die, and each die is a near perfect six-sided cube, guaranteed to be within 1/10,000 of an inch accurate.

Each die has six equally possible outcomes when thrown - numbers one through six. The two dice thrown together have a total of 36 possible outcomes, the six combinations of one die by the six combinations of the other.

The chart below shows these combinations.

Combinations of the Dice	
Result	Odds of Result
2	1 out of 36
3	2 out of 36
4	3 out of 36
5	4 out of 36
6	5 out of 36
7	6 out of 36
8	5 out of 36
9	4 out of 36
10	3 out of 36
11	2 out of 36
12	1 out of 36
Total	**36 out of 36**

You can see by the chart that the 7 is more likely to be thrown than any other number, having six possible combinations.

Next in frequency are the 6 and the 8, five outcomes each, then the 5 and the 9, four outcomes, the 4 and the 10, three outcomes apiece, the 3 and the 11, two outcomes, and finally, the 2 and the 12, one combination each.

A Shortcut to Remembering the Odds

Notice the symmetry of combinations on either side of the 7. The 6 and 8 have equal possibilities of being thrown, just as the 5 and 9, 4 and 10, 3 and 11, and 2 and 12 do.

If you take rolls of 7 and below and subtract one from that number, you arrive at the correct number of combinations for that roll. Thus, there are four ways to roll a 5 (5-1), six ways to roll a 7 (7-1) and one way to roll a 2 (2-1).

For numbers greater than the 7, match that number with the corresponding symmetrical number on the other side of the 7, and subtract one. Thus, to find the combinations of the 8, you match it with the 6 (which has an equal likelihood of occurring), and subtracting one, you get five combinations.

Figuring the Odds of Rolling a Specific Number

To figure the odds of rolling any particular number, divide the number of combinations for that particular number into 36, the total number of combinations possible.

Let's say the 7. There are six ways to roll a 7. Dividing the six combinations into 36, the total number of combinations, we find the odds of rolling a 7 on any one roll is one in six (6/36 reduced to 1/6), or equivalently, 5 to 1. The chart following shows the odds of rolling a number on any one roll.

Odds of Rolling the Numbers

The Roll	Combinations	Chance of Being Rolled	Odds Against
2 or 12	1	1/36	35 to 1
3 or 11	2	2/36	17 to 1
4 or 10	3	3/36	11 to 1
5 or 9	4	4/36	8 to 1
6 or 8	5	5/36	6.2 to 1
7	6	6/36	5 to 1

Understanding The Terminology-
Correct Odds, House Payoff and Edge

The house advantage or edge is the difference between the player's chances of winning the bet, called the **correct odds**, and the casino's actual payoff, called the **house payoff** or simply, the **payoff**. For example, the correct odds of rolling a 7 are 5 to 1. Since the house will pay only 4 to 1 should the 7 be thrown, they maintain an edge of 16.67 percent on this wager.

To play craps intelligently and better understand the choices available to him, the player must first and foremost be aware of the house advantage on every bet he will ever make, for that, in the long run, determines the player's chances of winning.

Five for One, Five to One

Sometimes on a layout you will see payoffs represented as *for* instead of the usual *to*, such as 9 for 1. This means that the payoff will be a total of nine units, eight winning chips along with your original bet, a house subterfuge to increase its edge over the player. The usual 9 to 1 payoff means nine winning chips and your original bet returned, for a total of 10 units.

Beware of any payoffs with the *for*. As a rule, this type of bet has poor odds to begin with and we wouldn't want to make it anyway, with the to or the for.

THE BETS

Craps offers the player a wide variety of possible wagers, with each bet having its own characteristics and inherent odds. Some bets, which we will refer to as **sequence bets**, may require a series of rolls before the outcome is determined, while the outcome of others, called **one-roll bets**, is determined on the very next roll.

Some bets are paid off by the house at **even-money**, for every dollar wagered, the player wins a dollar, while other bets have payoffs as high as 30 to 1. However, as you will see, generally the higher the house payoff, the worse the odds are.

And the odds of the bet, that is, the mathematical house return on every dollar wagered, is the most important concern of the player. To have the best chances of winning, you must avoid all the sucker bets, and make only the best bets available.

The Best Bets

The bets presented in this section have the lowest built-in house edge of all the bets in craps, and one bet, the free-odds bet, gives the house no advantage whatsoever. These bets, the pass, don't pass, come, don't come and the free-odds bets, are the most important bets a player can make, and are the foundation of our winning strategies.

THE LINE BETS - PASS AND DON'T PASS

These even-money bets can only be made on a come-out roll, before a point is established, and give the house an edge of only 1.4 percent. And when backed by the free-odds wagers, the overall house edge drops to 0.8 percent in a single odds game and to 0.6 percent in a double odds game.

Pass Line

Players making pass line bets are wagering that the dice will **pass**, or win, and are called right bettors. Pass line bets are also referred to as **front line bets**, and are made by placing the wager in the area marked *pass line*.

On the come-out roll, a throw of a 7 or 11 is an automatic winner for the pass line bettors while the throw of a craps, a 2, 3 or 12 is an automatic loser. If any other number is thrown, the 4, 5, 6, 8, 9 or 10, then that number is established as the **point**, and the shooter must repeat the point before a 7 is thrown for pass line bettors to win. The throw of a 7 before the point repeats is a loser for pass line bettors, called **sevening-out**, and the dealers will collect the lost bets.

Once the point is established, only the 7 and the point number affect the pass line bettor. All other numbers have no bearing on the bet and can be considered neutral throws.

Let's look at three progressions to see how the pass line bet works.

1. The come-out roll is a 5, establishing 5 as the point. The following roll is a 2, a neutral throw, for a point has already been established. An 8 is then thrown, also neutral, and then a 5. The point was repeated, or made, before the seven was thrown, and the pass line bettors win their bets.

2. The come-out roll is a 7, an automatic winner for the pass line bettors. Since the progression is completed, the following roll will be another come-out roll.

3. Here's a losing proposition. The come-out roll is a 9, establishing 9 as the point. The shooter then rolls a 6, 12, and 11, all neutral rolls since a point is already established. Then a 7 is thrown. Since the 7 was rolled before the 9, the shooter's point repeated, pass line bettors lose and the dealer will collect their bets. A new come-out roll will ensue.

Pass Line Capsulated

Payoff: Even -Money   **House Edge:** 1.4%
Automatic Winners - 7 or 11 on the come-out roll.
Automatic Losers - 2, 3, or 12 on the come-out roll.

Once a point is established, the pass line bettor:
Wins by the point repeating before the 7 is thrown.
Loses by the roll of a 7 before the point repeats.

Don't Pass

Players betting don't pass are called wrong bettors, and are betting against the dice. Don't pass bets are also called **back line bets** and are made by placing the wager in the area marked *don't pass*.

On the come-out roll, a throw of a 2 or 3 is an automatic winner for the don't pass bettors, while a 7 or an 11 is an automatic loser. The 12 is a standoff between the back line bettor and the house. (In some casinos the 2 is the standoff and the 12 is the automatic winner. Either way it makes no difference, for there is only one way to throw the 2 or 12.)

Once the point is established, don't pass bettors win by having the 7 thrown before the shooter repeats his point, and lose by the point being repeated before the shooter sevens-out. Here are some progressions to illustrate the don't pass wager.

1. The come-out roll is a 6, establishing 6 as the point. The following rolls are a 5 (no bearing on the outcome), then a 12 (still no bearing) and then a 7. Since the 7 was rolled before the 6 repeated, don't pass bettors win.

2. The come-out roll is a 3, an automatic winner for the don't pass bettor.

3. The come-out roll is a 4, establishing 4 as the point. A 3 is then rolled (neutral), and then a 4, a loss for the back line bettors since the point repeated before the 7 was rolled.

Don't Pass Line Capsulated

Payoff: Even-Money   **House Edge:** 1.4%
Automatic Winners - 2 (or 12) and 3 on the come-out roll.
Automatic Losers - 7 or 11 on the come-out roll.
Standoff - 12 (or 2 in some casinos) on the come-out roll.

Once a point is established, don't pass bettors:
Win by the throw of a 7 before the point repeats.
Lose by the point repeating before the 7 thrown.

COME AND DON'T COME BETS

The come and don't come bets work according to the same rules as the pass and don't pass bets except that the come and don't come bets can only be made *after* a point is established. The line bets, on the other hand, can only be placed on a come-out roll, before a point is established.

The advantage of these bets are that they allow the player to cover more points as a right or wrong bettor at the same low 1.4% house edge. And like the line bets, the overall house edge drops to 0.8% when backed by single odds, and 0.6% when backed by double odds.

Come bets are made by putting the chips into the area marked *come*, while don't come bets are placed in the *don't come box*. Won bets are paid at even-money.

Come Bets

We follow the play of the come bets just as we would with the pass line bets. A 7 or 11 on the first throw following the placing of the bet is an automatic winner, while a 2, 3 or 12 in an automatic loser.

Any other number thrown, the 4, 5, 6, 8, 9 or 10, becomes the point for that come bet, called the **come point**, and the dealer will move the bet from the come box into the large rectangular numbered boxes located at the top of the layout to mark the come point.

Once the come point is established, the bet is won if the come point repeats before the shooter sevens-out, and lost if the 7 is rolled before the point repeats. All other throws are inconsequential on this bet. Won bets will be paid off and removed from the layout.

The bettor can make continuous come bets until all the points are covered if he desires. Thus, it is possible for the throw of a 7 to simultaneously wipe out several established come bets. On the other hand, a hot shooter rolling point numbers can bring frequent winners to the aggressive come bettor.

Let's follow a progression where the right bettor makes both pass line and come bets.

Player Bets $5 on the pass line. *The come-out roll is a 5*, establishing 5 as the point.

Player Bets $5 on the come. *The roll is an 8*, establishing 8 as the come point. The dealer moves the $5 come bet to the rectangular box marked 8 to indicate that 8 is the point for that come bet. In effect, the player has two points working, the 5 and the 8, and decides to make another come bet.

Player Bets $5 on the come. *The roll is a 6*. The dealer moves this new bet to the 6, the come point for this bet. The other two points are not affected by this roll. The player has three points established, the 5, 6 and 8, and makes no more bets at this time.

The roll is a 5, a $5 winner on the pass line. It is paid off and removed from the layout, leaving the player with two come points, the 6 and 8.

Player Bets $5 on the pass line. Since the next roll is a come-out roll and the player wants to cover another point, he bets the pass. *The roll is a 10*, establishing 10 as the point.

Player makes no additional bets at this time. *The roll is a 2* (neutral on all established bets), then *an 8 is thrown*, a $5 winner on the come point of 8, and that bet is paid off and removed.

The following roll is not a come-out roll, for the come point was made, not the pass line point, the 10.

Player Bets $5 on the come. *The roll is a 7*. While the 7 is a $5 winner for the new come bet, it is a loser for the two established points, and they are removed from the layout by the dealer.

The roll of the 7 cleared the layout, and the following roll will be a new come-out roll.

Don't Come Bets

Like the don't pass wager, a 7 or 11 on the first roll following a don't come bet is an automatic loser and the 2 and 3 are automatic winners, 12 being a standoff. (In casinos where the 2 is a standoff and the 12 a winner on the don't pass, the same will hold true for the don't come bets.)

If a 4, 5, 6, 8, 9 or 10 is thrown, establishing a point for the don't come bet, the dealer will move the chips behind the appropriate point box to mark the don't come point. Don't come bettors now win by having the 7 thrown before that point is made. Other numbers, as with the don't pass bets, are neutral rolls. Only the 7 and the come point determine the bet.

Let's follow a progression where the wrong bettor makes both don't pass and don't come bets.

Player Bets $5 on the don't pass. *The roll is a 10*, establishing 10 as the point.

Player Bets $5 on the don't come, continuing to bet against the dice. *The roll is a 2*, a $5 winner on the new don't come bet, and that bet is paid off and removed.

Player Bets $5 on the don't come. *The roll is a 6*. The dealer moves the bet from the don't come area to the upper section of the box numbered 6 to indicate that 6 is the point for this don't come bet. The player now has two points working, the 10 and 6, and decides to establish a third point.

Player Bets $5 on the don't come. *The roll is a 10*, a $5 loser on the don't pass since the point repeated before a 7 was thrown. The don't come point of 6 is unaffected, and the new don't come bet is moved to the 10 box, since 10 is the come point for the new don't come wager.

The player decides not to make any more bets, but if he did, he would bet don't pass for the next throw is a come-out roll. *The roll is 7*, winner on both come points, and they are paid off and removed. The next roll will be a new come-out roll.

FREE-ODDS BETS

Though not indicated anywhere on the layout, the **free-odds** or **odds** bets are the best bets a player can make at craps, and are an indispensable part of any winning strategy. The free-odds bets are so named, for, unlike the other bets at craps, the house has no advantage over the player. Hence, the term *free-odds*.

However, to make a free-odds bet, the player must first have placed a pass, don't pass, come or don't come wager, and in a sense, is backing those bets, for the free-odds bet can only be made in conjunction with these wagers.

When backed by single odds, the overall odds of the pass, don't pass, come and don't come bets drop to 0.8%, and where double odds are allowed and utilized, the overall odds drop to only 0.6% against the player.

These are the best odds a player can get at craps.

Free-Odds - Pass Line

Once a point is established on the come-out roll, the pass line bettor can make a **free-odds bet**, and is betting that his point will repeat before a 7 is thrown.

This bet is paid off at the correct odds, giving the house no edge, and is made by placing the chips behind the pass line wager and just outside the pass line area.

Pass Line and Free-Odds Bet

When single odds are allowed, the player can bet up to the amount wagered on his pass line bet, and in certain instances he can bet more. And when double odds are allowed, the player can bet twice his pass line bet as a free-odds wager.

Though the player can bet less than the permissible amount on the free-odds wager and is allowed to reduce or remove this bet at any time, he should never do so, for the free-odds bets are the most advantageous bets in craps, and should be fully taken advantage of.

Following is a table which shows the correct odds of the point repeating before a 7 is thrown and the house payoff. Note how the house takes no percentage advantage on these bets since the payoff is identical to the correct odds.

Odds of Point Repeating Before a Seven

Point Number	Correct Odds	House Payoff
4 or 10	2 to 1	2 to 1
5 or 9	3 to 2	3 to 2
6 or 8	6 to 5	6 to 5

The odds presented in this table are easy to figure

for the only numbers that affect the free-odds bet are the point number, which is a winner, and the 7, which is a loser. All other throws are inconsequential.

There are three ways to roll a winning 4 or 10, and six ways to roll a losing 7, thus 2 to 1 is the correct odds on points 4 or 10. A 5 or 9 can be rolled four ways each against the same six ways of rolling a 7, thus the correct odds are 3 to 2 against the 5 or 9. A 6 or 8 can be made by five combinations, and again, since there are six ways to roll a losing 7, the correct odds are 6 to 5 against the 6 or 8.

Special Allowances - Single Odds Game

To make the payoffs easier, most casinos allow the player to make a single odds bet greater than his pass line (or come) bet in the following instances.

a. With a pass line bet such as $5 or $25 and the point being a 5 or 9, the casino will allow the player to make an odds bet of $6 and $30 respectively behind the line. If the bet is won, the 3 to 2 payoff on the $6 free-odds bet would be $9, and on the $30 bet, $45.

Without this special allowance, the player would be unable to get the full correct odds on the $5 or $25 free-odds bet since the $1 or more minimum craps tables do not deal in half dollars.

b. With a three unit bet such as $3 or $15, and the point being a 6 or 8, the casino allows a five unit free-odds bet behind the line thus permitting the player to take full advantage of the 6 to 5 payoff on points 6 and 8. In the above examples, $5 and $25 free-odds bets would be permitted, and if won, would pay the player $6 and $30 respectively.

A three unit bet translates to $3 for the $1 bettor,

$15 for the $5 bettor, $30 for the $10 bettor, and so on. Any bet that can be divisible by three can be considered a three unit bet and be backed by the special allowance single odds bets.

A $30 bet on the pass line can be backed by only $30 if the point is a 5 or 9 since the 3 to 2 payoff can be made on this amount, but if the point is a 6 or an 8, can be backed by $50 (five unit special allowance).

If uncertain about the amounts you are allowed to bet, check with the dealer, and he'll let you know the permissible wager.

No special allowances are allowed when the 4 or 10 are points for they are easily paid off at 2 to 1 no matter the amount wagered.

On bets smaller than $5 with the point being a 6 or 8, single odds bets will not receive the full 6 to 5 payoff, and will be paid off at even-money only, for again, the craps tables do not stock units smaller than $1 chips.

Three Unit Bet • Single Odds Special Allowance

Basic Three Unit Bet	6 or 8 as Point
$3	$5 ($6)
$15	$25 ($30)
$30	$50 ($60)
$45	$75 ($90)
$75	$125 ($150)
$300	$500 ($600)

The first column, *Basic Three Unit Bet*, is what our standard pass and come bet is, while the second column shows the special allowance permitted when the point is 6 or 8. Numbers in parenthesis indicate the amount paid if the single odds bet is won. Note that this is only a partial listing of the basic three unit bets.

On bets larger than $5 but in unequal multiples of $5, the free-odds bet will be paid to the highest multiple of $5 at 6 to 5, and the remainder will be paid at even-money. Thus, a $12 odds bet on the 8 will yield a payoff of only $14, $12 on the first $10 (at 6 to 5), and even-money on the unequal remainder of $2.

When the free-odds bets do not receive their full payoff, the bet works to the disadvantage of the player. Therefore, we recommend that pass and come wagers be made in multiples of $3, for this allows the player to take full advantage of the special allowances and lowers the overall house edge for the single odds game below 0.8%.

Double Odds - Pass Line

Double odds work just like single odds except that the player is allowed to bet double his pass line bet as a free-odds wager. If $10 was bet on the pass line and a 5 was established as the point, the double odds game allows the player to bet $20 as a free-odds wager and receive the same correct 3 to 2 odds on that point, instead of only being allowed a $10 free-odds bet as in the single odds game.

Special Allowances - Double Odds Game

One special allowance to keep in mind in double odds games. With a two unit bet on the pass line and the point a 6 or 8, double odds games allow the player to wager five units as a free-odds bet. Thus, with a $10 bet (two $5 unit chips), and the point a 6 or 8, a $25 double odds bet would be allowed. If won, the 6 to 5 payoff would bring $30 in winnings (six $5 chips, an easier payoff for the casino).

We recommend that players bet in multiples of two for it permits us to take advantage of the special five unit allowance when the point is a 6 or an 8. Any bet that can be divisible by two can be considered a two unit bet and be backed by the special five unit allowance if the point is a 6 or an 8.

Two Unit Bet • Double Odds Special Allowance

Basic Two Unit Bet	6 or 8 as Point	4, 5, 9 or 10 as Point
$2	$5 ($6)	$4
$10	$25 ($30)	$20
$20	$50 ($60)	$40
$30	$75 ($90)	$60
$50	$125 ($150)	$100
$200	$500 ($600)	$400

*The first column, Basic Two Unit Bet, is our standard pass and come bet. The second column is the special allowance bets permitted when the point is 6 or 8. The third column is the normal double odds allowance for points 4, 5, 9 and 10.

Numbers in parenthesis ( ) indicate the payoff if the double odds bet is won (at 6 to 5 payoff) when the point is 6 or 8. Other two unit bets are possible.

Free-Odds - Don't Pass

Once the point is established, don't pass bettors are allowed to make a free-odds bet that a 7 will be rolled before the point repeats. The bet is paid off at correct odds, the house enjoying no edge, and is made by placing the free-odds bet next to the don't pass wager in the don't pass box.

Don't Pass and Free-Odds Bet

Since the odds favor the don't pass bettor once the point is established, there being more ways to roll a winning 7 than any point number, the don't pass bettor must *lay odds,* that is, put more money on the free-odds bet than he will win.

Let's say the point is a 4. The don't pass bettor's chances of winning the bet are now 2 to 1 in his favor. There are only three ways to roll a 4, a loser, against the six combinations of a 7, a winner. Therefore, the don't pass bettor must bet $20 to win $10 when the point is a 4 (or 10).

(On the other side of the bet, pass line bettors are receiving 2 to 1 odds, for their bet is the underdog, having only three winning chances against six losing combinations.)

To lay odds as a don't pass bettor, the allowable free-odds bet is determined by the *payoff,* not the original bet. Using the above example of a $10 bet on the don't pass with 4 established as the point, the don't pass bettor in a single odds game is allowed up to a $10 win on the free-odds bet.

Since the odds are 2 to 1 in his favor, the don't pass bettor must lay $20 to win $10. If it was a double odds game, meaning the player could win $20 on his original $10 bet, than at 1 to 2 odds, $40 would have to be staked for a potential win of $20.

The odds the don't pass bettor must lay are exactly opposite the odds pass line bettors take on the same points. Below is a table showing the free-odds bets from the wrong bettors position.

Like the free-odds bets for right bettors, don't pass free-odds wagers can be removed or reduced at any time, but since these are the player's best bets, it should not be done.

Odds of Rolling a Seven Before Point Repeats

Point Number	Correct Odds	House Payoff
4 or 10	1 to 2	1 to 2
5 or 9	2 to 3	2 to 3
6 or 8	5 to 6	5 to 6

Note how the house has no percentage advantage on these bets since the payoff is identical to the correct odds.

Let's look at a quick example to see how the free-odds bet works for the don't pass bettor.

$10 is bet on the don't pass, and the *come-out roll is a 9*. The wrong bettor *bets $15* behind the line as a free-odds bet, the maximum allowed in a single odds game. He stands to win $10 on the $15 free-odds bet if the 7 is rolled before the 9 repeats (since he's laying 2 to 3 odds), in addition to $10 on his don't pass bet.

Should the point be rolled before the 7, the $15 free-odds bet and $10 don't pass bet will be lost. If double odds were allowed, $20 would be the maximum allowable free-odds win. At 2 to 3 odds, the don't pass bettor would have to lay $30 to win that $20.

Wrong Bettors Special Allowances - Single Odds

The casino makes a special provision for don't pass bettors when the point is a 5 or 9 and an odd figure such as $5 is wagered. Since the craps tables do not deal in half dollars, the player is allowed to make a free-odds bet of $9 behind the line in this instance, and if the bet is won, will get paid $6 ($9 at 2 to 3).

When the point is 5 or 9 and the original bet is unequal, the house allows the player to bet more than the straight single odds. Just ask the dealer the exact amount allowed in those instances for the rules may vary from casino to casino.

Free-Odds: Come and Don't Come

Once a come point is established, the bettor can take odds (or lay odds for don't come bettors) and get the same advantageous payoffs, 2-1 on points 4 and 10 (1-2 for wrong bettors), 3-2 on the 5 and 9 (2-3), and 6-5 on the 6 and 8 (5-6). The same special allowances apply for these free-odds bets.

The house has no advantage on these wagers, and like the line bets, the overall house edge on the come or don't come bets teamed with single odds drops to 0.8%, and with double odds, to 0.6%.

However, the odds bets on the come and don't come bets are placed differently than line bets. Rather than being made by the player, the odds bets are given to the dealer to place with the instruction, "odds on the come," or "odds on the don't come."

The dealer will place the odds bet in the appropriate box atop the come point, but slightly offset, so that the odds bet can be differentiated from the come bet.

Come, Don't Come and Free-Odds Bets

Dealer will place free-odds bet atop original bet but offset to distinguish from come or don't come bet.

		don't come and free-odds bet
8	NINE	10 come and free-odds bet

The only other difference is with the come bet. While the come bet itself is working on the come-out roll, the *odds bet on that come bet is not*. Let's say the player had $15 bet on the come point of 6 and had that bet backed by $25 free-odds. A come-out roll of a 7 would of course be a loser for the $15 come bet, as that bet is always working, but since the free-odds bet was off, the $25 single odds wager would be returned to the player.

If a 6 was rolled instead, a winner for the come bet, the player would only win the $15, and be returned the $25 odds bet.

Though it is standard procedure for the free-odds bet backing the come wager to be off on the come-out roll, the player can request the odds bet to be "on" by informing the dealer that the "odds are on for the come bet," and then, of course, the odds bet is subject to the normal rules.

The odds on the don't come bets, as with the pass and don't pass wagers, are always working.

THE REST OF THE BETS

With the exception of the place bet of 6 and 8, none of the bets presented in this section, which include the remainder of the bets possible at craps, are recommended for play. The house edge over the player on these bets is too large to be incorporated into a winning strategy, and the bettor making these bets will soon find himself drained of significant portions of his bankroll.

The bets listed in this section are discussed anyway so that you have a full understanding of all possibilities, and are never tempted to make these poor wagers.

Place Bets

The **place bets** are among the most popular wagers in craps, and are a bet that a particular point number, whichever is wagered on, the 4, 5, 6, 8, 9 or 10, is rolled before a 7 is thrown. The player can make as many place bets as he wants, and some players do, covering all the numbers with place bets.

However, this is not recommended strategy, for as we will see, with the exception of the place bets of 6 and 8, the other place bets, the 4, 5, 9 and 10, are poor wagers, and will have no role in our winning strategies.

Place bets are made by giving the dealer the desired wager, and telling him, for example, "to place the 9," or any such statement that indicates the player wants to make a place bet on the 9.

Though place bets can be made at any time, they are not working, or are "**off**" on the come-out roll, unless the player requests them to be "**on**" (working). The player can also request his place bets to be off for a limited series of throws, and may increase, reduce or remove them at any time prior to a roll.

House Payoffs on Place Bets			
Bet	Payoff	Correct Odds	House Edge
4 or 10	9 to 5	2 to 1	6.67%
5 or 9	7 to 5	3 to 2	4.00%
6 or 8	7 to 6	6 to 5	1.52%

To get the full payoffs on the place bets, the player should make his bets in the proper multiples. On place bets of 4 and 10, and 5 and 9, the bets should be made in multiples of $5 since the payoffs are 9 to 5 and 7 to 5 respectively. On the 6 and 8, the bet should be in multiples of $6 (7 to 6 payoff).

Excess bets in unequal multiples will be paid off at even-money only and work to the disadvantage of the player. For example, a $10 bet on the 6 will be paid as follows. The first $6 will get the full 7 to 6 odds for $7, while the remaining $4 gets paid at even-money, or $4, for a total win of $11. The last $4, paid off at only even-money, is a terrible payoff, and makes the entire bet a poor one.

Unless the player makes the place bets of 6 or 8 in multiples of $6 to insure full payoffs, the bet should not be made. Also, bets less than $5 on the 4, 5, 9 and 10, and less than $6 on the 6 and 8, will be paid of at only even-money.

To summarize, do not make place bets of 4 or 10, or 5 and 9, for the house edge is too high.

The place bets of 6 and 8 have playable odds of 1.52% and can be used in an aggressive maximize gain strategy, though some players may prefer to stick with the line, come and don't come bets backed by free-odds, the best bets of all.

Big 6 and Big 8

The **Big 6** and **Big 8** are bets that a particular number bet on, the 6 or 8, is thrown before a 7 is rolled. These bets can be made at any time, and are bet by putting the wager into the box marked Big 6 or Big 8.

These bets work just like the place bets of 6 and 8 except that the house only pays even-money on a won bet as opposed to the 7 to 6 payoff he would receive had he made the superior place bet on 6 or 8 instead. The house has a whopping 9.90% advantage on the Big 6 and Big 8 bets.

Buying the 4 or 10

This is an option the casino gives the player when betting on a place number, and though it reduces the odds on the 4 or 10 from 6.67% to 4.76%, the buy bet is still a poor one and should not be made. But here's how it works.

To **buy** the 4 or 10, you must give the house a 5% commission on your bet. Once you've bought a number, the house will pay off the bet at the correct odds. Thus, your payoff will be 2 to 1, the correct odds, rather than 9 to 5 as is usually the payoff for these place bets.

A 5% commission on $20 would be $1. For any bet smaller than $20, the commission would still be $1 since the craps tables generally carry no smaller units. In these cases, the house edge on your buy bet would be much larger than 4.76%. If you buy the 4 and 10 at $10 each, for a total of $20, the commission would only be 5% of the two bet total, or $1.

Like the place bets, buy bets are not working on the come-out roll, unless you instruct the dealer that the bet is on. They are also similar to the place bets in that they can be increased, reduced or removed at any time prior to the roll. Note that an increased buy bet is subject to the 5% commission on the additional wager.

Some casinos will keep the 5% commission if you decide to remove an established bet or charge an additional 5% if you win your bet and decide to let it ride.

Buying the 5, 6, 8, 9

Theoretically, you can buy these numbers as well, but since the commission is 5%, and the house edge on all these place bets is less than that, there is no advantage in buying these numbers.

Lay Bets

The **lay bet** is the opposite of a buy bet, and is used by wrong bettors who are wagering that the 7 will be thrown before the point or points they bet against is rolled. While the bet is paid off at correct odds, it costs the bettor 5% commission on the projected win to get this payoff, and is therefore, a poor bet.

Lay bets, which can be added to, reduced or removed altogether at any time, are made by giving the dealer your chips along with the required 5% commission on the projected win. The dealer will place the bet above the point number covered (in the area where the don't come bets are placed) and place a buy button on top to distinguish the lay bet.

To receive the full value on the lay bet of 4 or 10, the bettor would have to wager at least $40 to win $20 (1 to 2 odds). The 5% commission on the projected win of $20 would be $1. Any bet smaller than the $40 lay bet on the 4 or 10 would still be charged the minimum $1 commission (craps tables do not generally deal in currency smaller than $1 chips) making the house edge greater than the 2.44% advantage already built into this wager.

The 5 and 9 lay bets would require a minimum wager of $30 for the player to get the maximum value. The potential $20 win (laying odds at 2 to 3) would be charged $1 commission. The 6 and 8 bets would require a wager of $24 at 5 to 6 odds on a projected win of $20 to get full value from the commission. Any bet smaller than the projected win of $20 would still be charged the minimum $1 commission, and raise the overall house edge on the wager.

House Allowance on Lay Bets	
Points	House Advantage
4 or 10	2.44%
5 or 9	3.23%
6 or 8	4.00%

Field Bet

The **field bet** is a one roll wager that the next throw of the dice will be a number listed in the field box, the 2, 3, 4, 9, 10, 11 or 12. If one of the numbers not listed is rolled, the 5, 6, 7 or 8, then the bet is lost.

The field bet can be made at any time and is done by placing the wager in the area marked "Field".

At first glance, the bet seems attractive. There are seven winning numbers listed in the field box, and two of these numbers, the 2 and the 12, pay double if they are rolled. In some casinos, the 2 or 12 pays triple. The other winning numbers, the 3, 4, 9, 10 and 11 pay even-money.

However, there are 20 combinations (of the 5, 6, 7

and 8) that will beat us, and only 16 that will win, giving the house an edge of 5.55% when the 2 and 12 are paid at 2 to 1, and 2.70% when one is paid at 2 to 1 and the other at 3 to 1.

PROPOSITION, OR CENTER BETS

The **proposition**, or **center bets**, as they are sometimes called, are located at the center of the layout, and are made by either giving the chips to the dealer who will pass them along to the stickman, or, as with the hardways bet or craps-eleven bet, can sometimes be tossed directly to the stickman.

The central area of the layout is under the complete domain of the stickman, and though he will physically handle the placing and removing of bets in this area, it is with the dealer that the player will generally make his bets and receive his payoffs.

The proposition bets are the worst bets a player can make at craps and should never be made. The house advantage rages as high as 16.67% on some of these wagers. However, these bets are listed and their odds explained so that the reader will be fully conversant with all the wagers possible at craps.

Any Seven

This bet that the following roll of the dice will be a 7, is paid off by the house at 4 to 1 (5 for 1), and is among the worst bets a player can make. The house maintains an exorbitant edge of 16.67% over the player. Don't even make this bet in your dreams.

Any Craps

This bet, located at the bottom of the center layout and along its sides, is a bet that the following roll will be a craps - a 2, 3 or 12.

There are four ways to roll a winner. The 2 and 12 account for one way each, while there are two ways to roll a three. The other 32 combinations are losers, making the correct odds 8 to 1. The house only pays 7 to 1, giving them an 11.1% advantage.

2 or 12

This is a bet that the next roll of the dice will come up a 2, or a 12 if you bet that number, and is paid off by the house at 30 to 1. Of the 36 possible combinations of the dice, there is only one way of rolling a 2 or a 12, making the correct odds 35 to 1 against rolling either number. With only a 30 to 1 payoff, the house enjoys a hefty 13.69% advantage.

Sometimes a casino may only pay off at 30 for 1 (29 to 1), giving them an edge of 16.67%. This should make no difference to us for we won't go near that bet in either case.

3 or 11

This is a wager that the following roll will be a 3, or an 11, whichever you place your money on, and the house payoff is 15 to 1. Since there are only 2 ways to roll either number out of a possible 36 combinations, the correct odds are 17 to 1 (34 losers, 2 winners). The house edge is 11.1%. Where the payoff is 15 for 1 (14 to 1), this edge jumps to 16.67%.

Horn Bet

It takes four chips or multiples thereof to makes this bet. The horn bet is a four way bet that the next roll will be a 2, 3, 11 or 12, in effect combining four poor bets together. The house pays off the winning number at the normal payoffs (15 to 1 for the 3 or 11, and 30 to 1 for the 2 or 12), and deducts the other three losing chips from the payoff.

This sucker bet combines four losing wagers for a combined house edge of 11.1%, or 16.67% with the poorer payoffs discussed earlier. Never make this bet.

Hop Bet

This one roll wager, which does not appear on the layout, is generally made on a combination of the dice not otherwise offered on the one roll bets, such as 2, 3. If the bet is a pair such as 5, 5, the player will get the same payoff as the casino gives on the 2 or 12 bet (30 to 1 or 29 to 1). If the bet is a non-pair, such as 4, 5, which has two ways to win (4, 5; 5, 4), the payoff will be the same as on the 3 or 11 bet (15 to 1 or 14 to 1).

To make a hop bet, give your bet to the dealer or stickman, and call out for example "Hop 54", if the 5, 4 is the hop bet you wish to make. With the more generous payoff hop bets give the casino an edge of 13.39%, otherwise the edge is 16.67%. In either case, consider the bet a donation to the casino.

Craps-Eleven

The stickman will constantly exhort the player to make this horrendous bet, which is an appeal to bet the Any Craps and 11 bet simultaneously. We don't want to go near either bet by itself let alone together. Save your money for the show.

HARDWAYS

Whenever the numbers, 4, 6, 8 or 10 are rolled as doubles, the roll is said to be thrown **hardways**. A throw of 2-2 is said to be **4, the hardway** or **hard 4**, and similarly with 3-3, 4-4 and 5-5 for hard 6, 8 and 10 respectively. Rolling the 4, 6, 8 and 10 in other combinations is called **easy** such as 6-4; *10 the easy way*.

Betting hardways is betting that the particular number you choose comes up hard before it comes up easy or before a 7 is thrown.

Hard 4 and Hard 10

There is only one way to throw a hard 4 (2-2) or hard 10 (5-5), and eight ways to lose - six ways to roll a seven, and two ways to throw a 4 or 10 the easy way (1-3, 3-1, 6-4 and 4-6). The correct odds are 8 to 1 but the house only pays 7 to 1 for an advantage of 11.1%. This weak bet should never be made.

Hard 6 and Hard 8

There are a total of 10 losing combinations - the 6 ways to roll a 7, and 4 ways to roll a 6 or an 8 the easy way. There is only 1 way to throw the 6 or 8 the hardway. The correct odds of this hardway bet is 10 to 1 but the house only pays 9 to 1, a hefty 9.09% edge.

WINNING STRATEGIES: BETTING WITH THE DICE

We'll use only the best bets in our strategies - the pass line, come and free-odds wagers, wagers which give the player the best chances of winning, and lower the house edge to 0.8% in single odds games and 0.6% in double odds ones.

Built-in to the strategies are methods to turn average wins into big winning sessions without any risk of big losses.

Basic Conservative Strategy - Single Odds

Our standard bet will be in increments of three units so that we can take advantage of the special free-odds allowances should the points be 6 or 8, whereupon we can back our pass line or come bet by five units, or points 5 or 9, where we can bet extra if the original bet is uneven such as $15, where $20 would be permitted as a free-odds wager.

This allows maximum usage of the free-odds bets, wagers the house has no edge on, and brings the overall house advantage down to the barest minimum possible in a single odds game.

These are the guidelines of the **Basic Conservative Strategy:**

1. We will make three unit pass line and come bets until we have two points established, and back both those bets with the maximum single odds allowed.

2. Every time a point repeats, whether as a come or pass line point, we will make another three unit pass line or come bet so that we continue to have two points working for us. If a 2, 3, 11 or 12 declares a winner or a loser on the new pass line or come bet, we will follow with another bet until we get that second point established and then take the maximum single odds allowed on that point.

3. If the shooter sevens-out, clearing the board of all bets, we'll begin the progression again with a new pass line bet.

Aggressive Strategy - Single Odds

Rather than playing only two points as in the **Basic Conservative Strategy**, this method immediately attempts to establish three points. Otherwise, all the principles and methods are the same.

With three points covered, the bettor using the **Aggressive Strategy** can make a lot of money when the shooter starts rolling numbers.

Double Odds Strategies

Whenever the bettor has a choice, he should always choose a double odds game over a single odds game, for the additional allowance of the free-odds bet drops the overall house edge from 0.8% to 0.6% when using our methods.

The playing strategies we will pursue in the double odds game are identical to the single odds game except that we will bet in units of two instead of units of three as recommended in the single odds game to take advantage of the special five unit free-odds allowance when the point is 6 or 8.

Basic Conservative Strategy bettors should establish two points with maximum double odds, while **Aggressive Strategy** bettors will want to cover three points. Follow the procedures for the single odds methods substituting only the two unit basic bet for the three unit bet, and making double odds bets instead of single odds.

Maximizing Profits - Double Odds Game

Again our strategy here will follow that of the single odds game except we'll be increasing our bets by two units instead of three.

Basic Conservative Strategy bettors won't begin increasing bets until they've accumulated 20 units in profits, and Aggressive bettors will need 25 units. Remember to take advantage of the special allowances when the point is a 6 or 8. A four unit bet can be backed by 10 units in the double odds game, and a six unit bet by 15.

When eventually the shooter sevens-out, ending our winning streak, we'll start the next progression again at two units, ready to capitalize on another hot roll should one develop.

WINNING STRATEGIES: BETTING AGAINST THE DICE

Though the odds of winning are equivalent to the right betting strategies, 0.8% in a single odds game and 0.6% in a double odds game, very few craps players bet against the dice. Many bettors feel uncomfortable about having to *lay odds*, putting more money on their free-odds bet than they'll win, but as stated earlier, the free-odds wagers give the house no edge betting right or wrong.

However, players betting against the dice don't mind laying odds, for the roll of a 7, their winner, will occur more often than any point number, and they'll have frequent winners.

In addition, should a point be repeated, a losing roll for wrong bettors, only one bet will be lost. The other points covered by the wrong bettor are still in play. On the other side of the dice, the right bettors fear the 7, for when it is thrown - boom - all their established points and free-odds bets are lost.

We will apply the same principles of play as right

bettors. We'll make only the best bets available to us, those that reduce the house edge to the lowest possible figure - the don't pass, the don't come and free-odds bets.

Basic Conservative Strategy
Single Odds Wrong Bettors

Our standard bet will be in even increments of two units. Bets such as $15 or $25 are difficult to work with when the point is a 5 or 9 and 2 to 3 odds should be laid. Betting in other unit sizes is equally valid, but the player will find it easiest to work in multiples of $10.

These are the guidelines of the **Basic Conservative Strategy:**

1. We will make two unit don't pass and don't come bets until we have established bets against two points, and back both those bets with maximum free-odds.

2. Should a point repeat, a loser for us, we will make another don't come or don't pass bet, so that we can continue to have bets working against two points. If a 2, 3, 11 or 12 determines a winner or loser on a new don't pass or don't come bet, we will follow with another bet until we get that second point established, and then we'll play the maximum single odds against that point.

3. Stop establishing don't pass and don't come bets if a second point repeats. This is an important safeguard to protect us against bad losing streaks.

4. If a 7 is thrown, a winner on all our bets, we'll begin the progression again with our two unit don't pass bet.

As cautious bettors, we'll limit ourselves to only two points and strictly follow the safeguards recommended in step 3.

Aggressive Strategy
Single Odds Wrong Bettors

Our **Aggressive Strategy** follows the same guidelines as the **Basic-Conservative Strategy** except that we'll cover three points during a shoot instead of two, and will stop making additional don't pass and don't come bets if three points repeat, instead of two as advised in the **Basic Conservative Strategy**.

We'll use the same bets - the don't pass, don't come and free-odds bets, and enjoy the same low 0.8% house edge as in a single odds game.

Double Odds Strategy - Wrong Bettors

Whenever possible, the wrong bettor should play a double odds game over a single odds game, for it lowers the overall house edge from 0.8% to 0.6%.

And we always want to play with the best odds we can get - the lower the house edge, the greater our chances of winning.

By nature, the double odds strategies are more aggressive than the single odds games, and are more in tune for players whose temperament demands hotter action. The double odds bettor lays more to win more and therefore needs a larger bankroll than his single odds counterpart. Therefore, to play this strategy, the double odds bettor must feel comfortable with the larger bet levels.

Our double odds strategies are identical to the single odds methods, except that we're playing double odds instead of single odds. We'll begin by making a two unit don't pass bet, and backing that bet by double odds once a point is established.

Basic Conservative Strategy bettors will follow with

a don't come bet and lay double odds on both points while **Aggressive Strategy** bettors will make two more don't come bets backed by the full double odds.

Like the single odds strategies, **Basic Conservative Strategy** players attempt to keep two points working at all times while **Aggressive Strategy** players strive for three working points.

When points repeat, new don't pass or don't come bets are made to reestablish another point, but should a second point repeat for **Basic Conservative Strategy** players or a third point for **Aggressive Strategy** players, then we'll curtail all new betting until the shooter sevens-out, a winner on our remaining bets.

We employ this stop-loss as a safeguard to protect against one really bad shoot wiping out our table stakes. However, should the dice start blowing profits in our direction, we're immediately ready to capitalize on the situation.

We start the next come-out roll fresh, with a two unit don't pass wager, always ready for the streak that will mint chips for us.

WINNING AT ROULETTE

INTRODUCTION

Roulette offers player a huge variety of bets, more than any other casino table game, and the constant possibilities of winning and the different payoffs of the wagers, ranging from even-money payoffs to returns of 35 to 1, keeps the game exciting and suspenseful.

We'll show you how to make all the different bets possible in roulette, the odds involved and how the game is played both here and abroad so that you'll be ready to play roulette anywhere in the world and be fully prepared to win!

THE BASICS OF ROULETTE

The Roulette Wheel

Roulette is played with a circular wheel containing 36 grooved slots numbered from 1 to 36, half the numbers of which are black and the other half red, a tiny ball which is used in conjunction with the wheel, and a betting layout where players can place their wagers.

In addition to the 36 numbers on the roulette wheel, the American game has a 0 and 00, while the European game has but one 0. The zero slots are neither red nor black as are the other numbers but are green in color.

The American Wheel

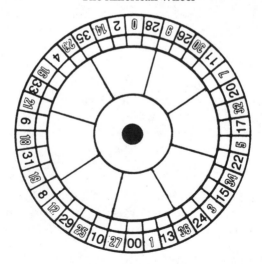

The wheel is cut into tiny pockets, one for each number - 37 total on a European wheel and 38 on an American - so that the ball, when spun around the wheel, will eventually fall into one of these slots - that number being the winning spin.

The Layout

The European game generally has the wheel flanked on two sides by a betting layout, so that the busy tables can accommodate players on both sides of the wheel, while the less popular American games typically use but one layout to the side.

The Dealer

The American game typically employs just one dealer who handles all of the functions at the table. He changes money into chips, spins the wheel, collects losing bets and pays off the winners. In between he finds time to stack and restack collected chips from the layout into neat, colorful piles, so that payoffs from the next spin will proceed smoothly and rapidly.

If a table is exceptionally busy, the dealer may have an assistant to help run the game.

European style games have one to as many as three or four **croupiers**, the French term for dealers, paying and collecting bets on the two adjacent layouts, and a **tourneur**, whose main responsibility is to spin the wheel and call the result. Often, a supervisor will be present as well.

Thus, when things get rolling and the tables crowded, one might find as many as six casino personnel manning a roulette game - a tourneur, four croupiers and a supervisor.

The Roulette Layout

1to18 EVEN	◇ ◆	ODD 19to36	1st 12	2nd 12	3rd 12	0		00
						1	2	3
						4	5	6
						7	8	9
						10	11	12
						13	14	15
						16	17	18
						19	20	21
						22	23	24
						25	26	27
						28	29	30
						31	32	33
						34	35	36
						2-1	2-1	2-1

The Play of the Game

Once players have placed their bets on the layout, choosing from the myriad possibilities available in front of them, the game is officially ready to begin. The roulette wheel will be spun by the dealer or tourneur who immediately afterwards, will throw the ball in the opposite direction from which the wheel is spinning so that both ball and wheel are racing in opposite directions on the wheel itself.

Players must now get in their last minute wagers for when the ball is about to leave the track, the dealer will announce that bets are no longer permitted. The call of *Faites vos jeux, messieurs* (Make your bets gentlemen) or *Rien ne va plus* (Nothing more goes) are classic in the French speaking casinos.

Once the ball has stopped, the dealer or tourneur will call out the outcome, and a marker will be placed on the number just spun so that all players and dealers can clearly see the winning number.

The dealers or **croupiers**, as they're called in French, will now settle the wagers. Lost bets are collected first by the dealers, and after this is done, all the winning bets will be paid off.

The Chips

Keeping track of one's bets are easy in American roulette games, for each player is issued special chips applicable only to the roulette game at that casino, and these chips are colored, a different color for each player. Ten different players may be represented by, for example, yellow, red, pink, blue, green, black, white, beige, purple and grey chips.

The colored chips are valid and can be used only

at the roulette table which issues them. If the table is crowded and no more colors are available, a player may use regular casino chips for his or her bets.

There is no confusion in ownership of the chips this way. Color coding makes life easy at these tables. When a player approaches the roulette table, he exchanges cash or casino chips for an equivalent value in the colored chips, called in the parlance of the game, **wheel checks**. The value assigned to those colored chips, be it 25¢, $1.00, $5.00 or whatever, is set by the player. Thus, if the player wants to value the chips at 25¢, more chips will be issued from the dealer than if the chips were valued at $1.00.

The dealer will place a coin or **marker button** on top of the colored chips and place these on the stationary outer rim of the wheel, so that the value of that wheel check is clearly marked.

When a player is ready to leave, he converts the wheel checks back into the regular casino checks with the dealer at that table.

Life is a bit more complicated in the European style game where color coding is not used and bettors simply use casino chips or cash to make their bets. Sometimes, in the confusion of a crowded game, vociferous arguments ensue as players lay identical claim to chips on the felt.

The Basic Odds

The primary difference in the popularity of European and American roulette lies in the simple fact that the European game gives the player much better odds of winning, and this is where the 0, 00 difference of the two wheels comes into play.

Let's see how the odds are figured.

There are slots numbered from 1 to 36 on the roulette wheel - a total of 36. There is only one way to win for each number chosen. That leaves 35 other numbers, which if they come up, are losers for the bettor. True odds of 35 to 1 against - 35 ways to lose, one way to win.

And that's exactly what the casino will pay on a single number bet. So where is the casino's profit?

It is the zeros added to the wheel that give casinos their edge, for now there are a total of 37 possibilities on a European wheel (single zero added) and 38 possibilities on an American one (double zero added). The casino's payoff is still 35 to 1, being based on the true odds of a 36 number wheel. However, with the added zeros, the true odds on a single number bet are now 36 to 1 on a single zero wheel (the European game) and 37 to 1 on a double zero wheel (the American game).

Those zeros give the casino its edge on all bets made. Unless the zero (and in American roulette the 00 also) are bet directly, the spin of either on the wheel causes all other wagers to lose.

The sole exceptions are the even-money bets in a European style game (and Atlantic City), for the spin of a zero gives the red-black (rouge-noir), high-low (passe-manque) and odd-even (impair-pair) bettors a second chance, and reduces the house edge on these bets to 1.35% (2.63% in Atlantic City) - the best odds one can receive in roulette.

The zeros represent the house advantage and that is why the 00 in American roulette makes that game a worse gamble for the player than its European counterpart. Atlantic City makes up for this a little by offering surrender on even-money bets, bringing the casino's edge on these wagers down to 2.63%.

Let's sum up the odds for you in chart form so that you can clearly see them in one spot.

Casino Edge in Roulette

American Roulette (Double Zero)	House Edge
The 5-Number Bet	7.89%
All Other Bets	5.26%
Atlantic City - Even Money Bets	2.63%
European Roulette (One Zero)	
Even-Money Bets - En Prison Rule	1.35%
All Other Bets	2.70%

The difference between the 1.35% of European style roulette and 5.26% of the American style is significant, almost a four-fold increase, which calculates directly to a loss rate four times as fast.

Now you can see why roulette with a single zero and en prison rule is the rage of Europe, and double zero American roulette is less popular.

THE BETS

Roulette offers the player a multitude of possible wagers, more than any other casino table game. All in all, there are over 150 possible combinations to bet. A player may make as many bets in whatever combinations desired as long as the bets fit within the minimum and maximum limit of the casino.

Let's now examine the bets one by one. (The

French terms for the bets are listed in the parenthesis.)

COMBINATION OR INSIDE BETS

These bets are made within the numbers on the layout, and hence, are termed *inside bets*.

Single Number Bet - (En Plein)

A **single number bet** can be made on any number on the layout including the 0 and 00. To make this wager, place your chip within the lines of the number chosen, being careful not to touch the lines. Otherwise you may have another bet altogether.

The winning payoff is 35 to 1.

The Single Number Bet

Split Bet (A Cheval)

Place the chip on the line adjoining two numbers. If either number comes up, the payoff is 17 to 1.

Split Bet (A Cheval)

4	5	6
7	8	9

Trio Bet (Transversale)

The chip is placed on the outside vertical line alongside any line of numbers. If any of the three are hit, the payoff is 11 to 1.

Trio Bet (Transversale)

4-Number Bet (Carre)

Also called a square or corner bet. Place the chip on the spot marking the intersection of four numbers. If any of the four come in it is an 8 to 1 payoff.

4-Number Bet (Carre)

Quatre Premiere

Only in European roulette. The bet covering the 0, 1, 2 and 3. An 8 to 1 payoff.

5-Number Bet

Only in American roulette. Place the chip at the intersection of the 0, 00 and 2 to cover those numbers plus the 1 and 3. If any of these five come home, the payoff is 6 to 1. In American roulette, it is the only bet not giving the house an edge of 5.26%. It's worse - 7.89%!

5-Number Bet

6-Number Bet (Sixaine)

Also called a **block bet**. The chip should be put on the outside line of the layout while intersecting the line separating the sets of numbers chosen. The payoff is 5 to 1.

6-Number Bet (Sixaine)

28	29	30
31	32	33

OUTSIDE BETS

These bets are outside the 36 numbers on the layout, and are aptly called, the outside bets. These include the columns, dozens and even money bets - red-black, high-low and odd-even.

Outside Bets

1st 12		2nd 12		3rd 12	
1to18	EVEN	◇	◆	ODD	19to36

Columns Bet (Colonne)

A chip placed at the head of a column, on the far side from the zero or zeros, covers all 12 numbers in the column and has a winning payoff of 2 to 1.

The 0 and 00 are not included in this bet and would be a loser if they come up.

Columns Bet (Colonne)

3	6	9	12	15	18	21	24	27	30	33	36	2-1
2	5	8	11	14	17	20	23	26	29	32	35	2-1
1	4	7	10	13	16	19	22	25	28	31	34	2-1

Dozens Bet (Douzaine)

This is another way to bet 12 numbers, either numbers 1 to 12, 13 to 24 or 25 to 36. On the American layout they're called the **first**, **second** and **third dozen** respectively, and on the French layout, they're known as **P12**, **M12** and **D12**. The winning payoff as in the column bet is 2 to 1.

Dozens Bet (Douzaine)

1st 12 ●	2nd 12 ●	3rd 12 ●

EVEN-MONEY BETS

There is one final type of bet, the even money bets: **Red-Black** (Rouge-Noir), **High-Low** (Passe-Manque) and **Odd-Even** (Impair-Pair). Spots for these bets are found outside the numbers, thus classified as *outside wagers*.

These wagers are clearly marked in large boxes.

In Atlantic City and European style roulette, these bets are the best at the roulette table, for they offer the player additional features which are greatly advantageous. In Europe, the features are called *en prison* and *partage*, and in Atlantic City, *surrender*.

Even-Money Bets

1to18	EVEN	◇	◆	ODD	19to36

Red-Black (Rouge-Noir)

There are 18 black and 18 red numbers. A player may bet either the **red** or the **black** and is paid off at 1 to 1 on a winning spin.

Red-Black (Rouge-Noir)

High-Low (Passe-Manque)

Numbers 1-18 may be bet (**low**) or 19-36 (**high**). Bets are paid off at 1 to 1.

High-Low (Passe-Manque)

Odd-Even (Impair-Pair)

A player may bet on the 18 even numbers (**even**) or on the 18 odd numbers (**odd**). Winning bets are paid at 1 to 1.

Odd-Even (Impair-Pair)

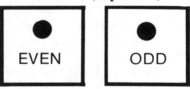

En Prison and Partage

It is on these even number bets - Red-Black, High-Low and Odd-Even - where the American and European games really differ. In American roulette, the house automatically wins on these bets when the 0 or 00 is spun (except in Atlantic City). However, in Europe, if the 0 is spun, the **en prison** rule comes into effect. The player has two choices now.

He or she can either surrender half the bet, called **partage**, or elect to allow the bet to be "imprisoned" one more spin. If the spin is won, the bet stays intact and is "released" for the player to do what he or she will. If the spin is lost, so is the bet.

This rule is greatly advantageous to the player, and brings the odds down on these bets to 1.35% in favor of the casino as opposed to the 2.70% on the rest of the bets in the single zero game.

Surrender

In an attempt to get more gamblers to play roulette, the game in Atlantic City helps make up for the 00 of the American wheel by offering **surrender**, which is really partage by another name.

When a 0 or 00 is spun, players with bets on any of the even-money propositions lose only half the bet, "surrendering it," and keep the other half. This brings the house edge down to 2.63% on these bets.

American and European Roulette

The European and American game is pretty much the same besides the use of the French terms in Europe, and of course the American terms in the U.S. casinos.

However, there are two significant differences.

1. In addition to the 36 numbers on the roulette wheel, the American game has a 0 and 00, while the European game has but one 0.

2. The European game offers en prison and partage, rules greatly beneficial to the player. En prison and partage is not offered in American casinos, with the exception of Atlantic City where surrender (partage) is used.

The end result, as we showed earlier, is that the casino edge in the European game is but 1.35% as opposed to American roulette where the player has to overcome a hefty 5.26% house edge (or 2.63% on even-money bets in Atlantic City).

WINNING STRATEGIES

First it must be stated clearly, that like most other casino games, the casino has the mathematical edge over the player, and that no betting strategy or playing system can overcome those odds unless the wheel is a biased one - which we'll cover.

That edge is 5.26% in American roulette, with the exception of even-money bets in Atlantic City where the edge is 2.63%, and 2.70% in European roulette, unless the even-money wagers are made, where the house edge drops to 1.35%.

Based on the above facts, one must develop a clear picture on how to approach a winning strategy.

Roulette Payoff Chart

Bets in Roulette

American Name	#	French Name	Payoff
Single Number	1	En Plein	35 - 1
Split Bet	2	A Cheval	17 - 1
Trio	3	Transversale	11 - 1
4-Number (Corner)	4	Carre	8 - 1
(Not Applicable)	4	Quatre Premiere	8 - 1
5-Number	5	(Not Applicable)	6 - 1
6-Number or Block	6	Sixaine	5 - 1
Columns Bet	12	Colonne	2 - 1
Dozens Bet	12	Dozaine	2 - 1
Red or Black	18	Rouge ou Noir	1 - 1
High or Low	18	Passe ou Manque	1 - 1
Odd or Even	18	Impair ou Pair	1 - 1

 # column is the amount of numbers covered by the bet.

First of all, it must be understood that in the long haul, the casino's edge will grind out the player - but that doesn't mean the player can't show a profit in the short run. Fluctuations are normal to gambling, whatever the game, and with a little luck, a player can ride a hot streak into some healthy profits.

There are many betting systems that have been

devised to overcome the casino's edge in roulette, but you must keep these in perspective, for they can no more alter or change the built-in house edge than one constantly calling a tree a river will change that tree to a river or calling blue red will change blue to red.

This is not to say that some of the betting strategies don't look good - some of them are brilliant in concept and *appear* foolproof. As long as one realizes the risks involved and understands that no strategy can negate the built-in house edge, betting strategies can be a lot of fun.

Betting strategies can work - in the short run - and provide the player with a fun, working approach to winning, and really, that's what the game is all about.

Let's look at one of the most famous systems first, The Martingale.

The Martingale

This dangerous system can dig you into a deep hole quick should you have a long string of losses - if not, like other systems, you'll be sitting pretty.

The system is easy. You attempt to win $1.00 on every sequence of the wheel, a sequence being defined as either one spin when you have won, or a number of spins, ending when there is a winner.

Your first bet is $1.00. If the bet is won, you start again, betting $1.00. If you lose, the bet is doubled to $2.00. Should that bet be won, you have won $1.00 on the sequence, a $1.00 loss on the first spin a a $2.00 win on the second. If the second bet is lost, the next bet is again doubled, and is now $4.00. A winner here again brings a $1.00 profit, $1.00 + $2.00 in losers for $3.00 total, and a $4.00 winner. Still $1.00 over the top.

And so the system works. Every won bet is followed by a $1.00 wager, the beginning of a fresh cycle. Every lost bet is followed by a doubling of that bet. And here is the danger of the Martingale. As consecutive losses mount, so does the size of your bet, where the end result is only a $1.00 win!

This is what happens if you lose seven in a row.

Martingale Progression		
Loss	Bet	Total Loss
1st	$1.00	$1.00
2nd	$2.00	$3.00
3rd	$4.00	$7.00
4th	$8.00	$15.00
5th	$16.00	$31.00
6th	$32.00	$63.00
7th	$64.00	$127.00
8th	$128.00	-

Now suddenly, you're faced with a $128.00 bet with $127.00 worth of losses behind you. Now that's a lot of sweat and aggravation just to win $1.00 on the sequence. And we all know that seven losses in a row is not that strange of an occurrence.

What happens on the next spin? Surely you're due for a winner now after seven consecutive losses. If you're pregnant or expecting a raise or some such thing, you may be due.

In gambling, you're never due for anything. There are expectations based on the odds, but the fact that seven times the wheel spun black when you've been betting red, has no bearing on the eighth spin. The odds don't change - it's still an 18 out of 37 (European wheel) or 38 (American wheel) shot for your winning red on the next spin.

Remember, it's only a wheel. It has no memory, no brain. It doesn't know who you are, what you're betting, or that seven times in a row, black came up on it.

So back to the game. Heaven forbid that two more spins should go against you, for then you'll be faced with the following:

Martingale Progression Continued		
Loss	**Initial Bet**	**Total Loss**
8th	$128.00	$255.00
9th	$256.00	$511.00
10th	$512.00	-

Add up these numbers than get out the Pepto-Bismol. Think twice before using this classic system. Do you really want to risk a situation where you'll need to bet over five hundred dollars just to win $1.00?

The Grand Martingale

If you liked the above example, you'll love this system. The rallying point of the **Grand Martingale** is to attempt to win more than $1.00 on a losing progression by adding $1.00 to the bet after each loss. We'll spare ourselves the anguish of adding up these numbers, but you can see they'll add up even faster than the Martingale, and should things go badly, the bets get scary in a real hurry.

The Pyramid System

This system is far more appealing to the player for its winning approach doesn't entail the kind of deep ditch digging that the Martingale and Grand Martingale do.

In this system, also called the **D'Alembert**, we'll look at each bet it terms of units, and to make life easy, we'll use $1.00 as our unit bet. The first bet will be $1.00. If we win, the sequence is ended, and we'll begin a new one.

If the bet is lost, our next bet becomes $2.00. Each subsequent loss adds $1.00 to the bet, so that five consecutive losses would produce a $6.00 bet on the following play. (Compare this to the Martingale, where you'd be watching a $32.00 bet gracing the tables for your $1.00 win, and the first tinges of a headache beginning to pound your skull.)

This system is interesting for after every win, you will decrease your bet by one unit! The end result of this system is that every win (as opposed to every progression) produces a win of $1.00, or if you prefer to think in terms of units, every win produces a one unit gain.

Every won bet is $1.00 more than the previous lost bet.

Let's follow a progression to see how this works.

Pyramid Progression		
Bet	**Result**	**Total**
$1.00	Win	+$1.00
$1.00	Loss	$0.00
$2.00	Loss	-$2.0
$3.00	Win	+$1.00
$2.00	Win	+$3.00
$1.00	Loss	+$2.00
$2.00	Loss	+$0.00
$3.00	Loss	-$3.00
$4.00	Loss	-$7.00
$5.00	Loss	-$12.00
$6.00	Win	-$6.00
$5.00	Loss	-$11.00
$6.00	Win	-$5.00
$5.00	Win	$0.00

TOTAL - 14 Plays: 6 Wins, 8 Losses

You can see the attractions of this system, for despite sustaining five straight losses and eight overall as against only six wins, the sequence where we left off showed the player dead even. A win on the next play would forge a profit of $4.00, with the next bet being $3.00, so the bettor's position looks pretty good overall.

This is all well and good on a short run look. However, in the long run, this system like all others trying to fight a game where the house has an edge, will ultimately lose. As the progression continues, there will be more losses than wins and the downward dips will be deeper and more frequent than wins.

As long as this is kept in mind, the immovable house edge, than one might play this system to great enjoyment, and in the short run, maybe some profit!

Biased Wheels

There is a way to beat the casino at roulette, but this involves finding an imbalanced wheel, presumably old and rickety, more likely in a smaller casino, or perhaps at a fair where the mechanics of the wheel are far from state of the art.

It is impossible to make a perfectly balanced wheel, one where each number has exactly the same chance of coming up as any other number. A slight imperfection in the material, normal wear and tear, a warp, a tiny tilt, an unlevel floor, a slightly larger or shorter slot - these possibilities or any of a number of others can cause an imbalance of a wheel and favor some numbers to be spun more than others.

Wheels are made with such tremendous precision nowadays that it is extremely unlikely to find a wheel with a bias significant enough to make this theory interesting.

However, you may find an older wheel in use, one that's been subjected to enough wear and tear of normal usage that a bias is created, or one with faulty mechanics, and until the casino has figured out that you've got something going on and shuts down the wheel, you can make a lot of money - with the odds.

First you must determine if the wheel is biased and how large the bias is. To do this requires a lot of work and patience, but if indeed your hunch is right and the wheel is significantly biased, you will have made the effort worthwhile.

To properly track a wheel, you'll need a partner or an associate or two for every spin of the wheel will need to be recorded for at least 24 hours to get a fair sampling. A sampling taken for less than 24 hours will only show short run deviations (unless the wheel is incredibly biased) and may not be an accurate look at biased numbers.

The expectation of any single number being spun is one in 37. For a bias to be effective and show profits, a single number's bias must not only be greater than the 1/37 expected result, but be sufficient enough to overcome the inherent casino's edge of 5.26% on an American wheel and 2.70% on a European one for single zero betting.

You may find one number or several that stand out on a wheel as being biased and base your winning strategy on those numbers (or number). The superior odds inherent in single zero roulette make those games much better to track for if a bias is found, the smaller house edge is easier to overcome and the profits will be greater.

WINNING AT SLOTS

INTRODUCTION

These ever-popular machines can be found around the world, buzzing, clanging and spitting out rewards to their faithful players. Millions are hooked on the game. Some play for the sheer pleasure, hoping to pass a little time and win a few coins, others play for that elusive thing, the big jackpot, which will set them on *easy street*.

In this section we'll show the basics of slots play including the different types of machines available, the percentage returns and payoffs, and of course, some strategy tips for winning big jackpots!

Let's now take a closer look at the game of slots and the exciting possibilities it holds in store for you.

The History of Slots

Charles Fey is credited with being the originator of slot machines in their more or less current format. His original machines, called **Liberty Bells**, were introduced in the late 1800s and first began to appear in the bars and saloons around the San Francisco Bay. There were coin-operated machines before Fey which were based on games of chance such as dice and roulette, but Fey's Liberty Bell was the first to feature a three reel design with automatic payouts to the winners.

These early machines used three reels of ten symbols each, among which were the famous Liberty Bell figures, along with other symbols of the times such as horseshoes. If the 10 possibilities per reel are multiplied by three reels, 10 x 10 x 10, we come up with 1,000 different possible combinations on these early machines.

Fey set the machines to pay back 86% to the players. The other 14%, the profit, he split 50-50 with the bar and saloon owners. The machines really took off and spurred a host of competitors, most notably Herbert Stephen Mills and the Caille Brothers. Slots have come a long way since then and account for important parts of a casino's income.

Nowadays, names such as Bally and International Game Technology are the big players and the old 5¢ machines, though still to be found, have given way to 25¢, $1.00 and even $100 slots!

TYPES OF MACHINES

There are basically two types of slot machines. The first type, the **Straight Slots**, pays winning combinations according to the schedule listed on the machine itself. For example, one cherry may pay two coins for each one put in, two cherries may pay five coins and three cherries 10 coins.

There are also **Progressive Slots** machines. These too have a standard set of payoffs listed on the machine itself, but in addition, and what sometimes makes for exciting play, is the big jackpot which progressively gets larger and larger as every coin is put in. The jackpot total is posted above the machine and can grow to enormous sums of money.

THE BASICS OF PLAY

Slots are easy to play. Machines generally take anywhere from 1 to 5 coins, and all one needs to do is insert the coins into the machine, pull the handle and see what Lady Luck brings.

There are many types of slot machine configurations but all work according to the same principles - the paying combinations that are always posted on the machine itself must be lined up in the window for a winner.

Often, the number of lines the machine will pay on depends on the amount of coins deposited. One coin only may pay the middle line, a second coin will pay the top line as well, a third coin - the bottom line, so now any of the three horizontals will pay should a paying combination be hit. A fourth coin may pay the diagonal, and a fifth, the other diagonal.

If the proper combination is hit, the machine should make a little noise for you as coins automatically pour into the well at the bottom. And should a really large payoff be hit, a **jackpot**, the machines will make a bunch of noise, a light may go off atop the machine and you just hang tight, for a casino employee should be there soon to give you the payoff.

More winning rows played does not necessarily equate to better odds of winning.

The odds are built into the machine and no amount of lines played will change them.

The most important factor affecting your chances at winning and the percentages at which you're gambling is how loose or tight the machines are set by the casino - that is what determines the odds facing a slots player.

Sample Slots Payoff
(per one coin)

Winning Combination	Payoff
7-7-7	100 coins
Bar-Bar-Bar	50 coins
Bell-Bell-Bell	20 coins
Bell-Bell-Bar	18 coins
Bar-Bell-Bell	18 coins
Plum-Plum-Plum	20 coins
Plum-Plum-Bar	14 coins
Bar-Plum-Plum	14 coins
Orange-Orange-Orange	20 coins
Orange-Orange-Bar	10 coins
Bar-Orange-Orange	10 coins
Cherry-Cherry-Cherry	20 coins
Any-Cherry-Cherry	5 coins
Cherry-Cherry-Any	5 coins
Cherry-Any-Cherry	5 coins
Any-Any-Cherry	2 coins
Cherry-Any-Any	2 coins

SLOT PERCENTAGES

The percentage return of slot machines vary from casino to casino, and often within a casino as well. While the Nevada regulatory commission sets no minimum at all, the Atlantic City gaming commission requires a minimum return of 83% back to the players. Within these loose frameworks, a whole range of percentages may apply.

In general, a casino that relies on slots for a good portion of their income will offer players a higher return on their slots money, while those that have the slots as but an incidental income, will pay less on the average.

Some casinos advertise slots with returns as high as 97% to the player, others, even as high as 99%! Obviously, the player stands a much better chance of winning at these places than others where a standard return of only 83% might be the norm. On machines in areas not covered by regulatory minimums, such as Nevada, players may not even get an 83% return.

WINNING STRATEGIES

The most important concept in slots is to locate the machines with the loosest setting, or with progressive machines, to play only the machines with the highest progressive setting.

The first thing to look for are casinos which really push their slot machine business and cater to the players, and also casinos which advertise a higher return. These are places that may offer slot players a better than average return.

In general, the poorer paying machines will be

located in areas where the casino or proprietor hopes to grab a few of the bettor's coins as he passes through an area or waits on a line. Airport terminals, restaurant and show lines, bathrooms and the like tend to have smaller returns.

On the other hand, casinos that specialize in slots and look to attract serious players, will set up slots areas within a casino that will have better payoffs, or even, as you can find in Las Vegas, the whole casino will be slots only! These casinos view slots as an important income, and in order to keep regular slots customers, their players must hear those jackpot bells ringing - after all, winning is contagious!

Some machines are set to pay better than others, and these slots will be mixed in with poorer paying ones, so its always a good idea to look for the hot machine. Better yet, ask the change girls. They spend all day near the slots and know which machines tend to return the most money.

Basically, your best strategy is to examine the wide array of machines offered for play, and to find the best one suited to your personal style.

When you hit a good jackpot, make sure you set your stop-loss limit. This guarantees that you walk away a winner!

WINNING AT VIDEO POKER

INTRODUCTION

Video poker is a lot of fun, for decision-making and skill are involved and even better, proper play can bring you profits! The game can be as leisurely or hurried as you want for there is no dealer to hurry you along. You choose your own pace - it's just you against the machine. May the best one win!

The whole setting is really simple. All one needs is some coins to play and an available video poker machine, and you're in business.

This section shows you the basic rules of play, how to work the video poker machines, the different machines available, the payoffs and winning hands, and most importantly, a winning strategy to arm you with the best odds and make you a winner.

PLAYER ADVANTAGE IN VIDEO POKER!

There is a big reason for video poker's increasing popularity - with proper play you can actually have the edge over the casino, and like blackjack, have the expectation of winning money every time you play!

That's right, with proper strategy, you'll have the edge in video poker and if that isn't incentive to put a little study in the game and improve your odds, I'm not sure what is.

What we'll show you in this section is a simplified basic strategy that will improve your odds and get your game going in the right direction.

However, for those players serious about beating the house, you'll want to buy the advanced video poker strategy listed in the back. It takes you beyond the simplified basic strategy presented here and shows you the full Basic Strategy Charts, the advanced strategies, which machines to play for best results and overall, how to be a winner and play video poker for a profit.

THE TYPES OF MACHINES

Video poker offers the player a variety of machines from which to choose. The two basic types of video poker machines are the **Flat-Top** (or **Straight**) machines and the **Progressives**. The Flat-Tops offer set payoffs on all the hands won, with the payoffs proportionately larger for greater amounts of coins played. Thus, a winning payoff on two coins played will be exactly double that for the same winning hand with one coin played.

The one exception is for the royal flush, where a winning payoff will give the player a 4,000 coin return when five coins are played, as opposed to only 200,

400, 600 and 800 coins on a one, two, three and four coin play respectively. All other payoffs are in proportion.

Winning payoffs are posted on the machine, so you can see right off what you're up against.

The Progressive machines differ from the Straight or Flat Tops in that when a royal flush is hit with five coins played, the payoff is not a set amount but is based on a progressive total. This jackpot constantly increases until the royal is hit, when it will start again at a set amount, such as $1,000 on a 25¢ machine.

The Progressives can be exciting for jackpots go higher and higher, and now and again, a quarter machine will soar well into the $2,000+ range or even higher. However, like the Straight machines, the full five coins must be played to reap the full reward when the royal flush is hit.

There are different varieties of the video poker machines within the above classifications.

A player may find Jacks or Better, 10s or Better, Deuces Wild and Joker Wild, and these can be played as Straights or Progressives, depending upon what casino players find themselves in and what machines are offered.

We'll talk more about this later when we discuss each game individually.

HOW TO PLAY

Video poker is basically played as draw poker. The machine uses a 52 card deck which is played fresh after each hand. While you won't receive the same card within a play, for the machine will deal cards from the 52 card computer pack, the memory ends there as the deck is "reshuffled" after each deal.

To start, you need to insert anywhere from one to five coins into the machine. The choice is yours - play one or play five at your discretion. We will recommend that serious players insert the full five coins to get the best odds, but we'll go into that later.

If five coins are inserted, the machine will automatically deal a hand to you. However, if less than the maximum amount is inserted, you'll need to press the button marked **DRAW/DEAL** to receive your cards.

Five cards will show on the screen. These are your cards. You may keep one, some, all or none of the cards. It's your decision. To keep a card, press the button marked **"HOLD"** underneath the corresponding card you wish to keep. There will be five hold buttons, one for each card, and for each card you want to keep, you must press the hold button.

"HELD" will appear on the screen underneath each card or cards so chosen. The other cards, the ones you wish to discard, will not be kept by the machine.

What happens if you press the wrong hold button by accident or change your mind? No problem. Press the corresponding button again. If the card indicated "HELD," it will no longer do so and will not be held by the computer. If you change your mind press the button one more time, and again the "HELD" sign will come on the screen indicating that the card will be kept on the draw.

Until you press the draw button, it is not too late to change your strategy decision.

A player may keep all five original cards and does so by pushing the hold button under each card or he or she may discard all five original cards if so desired.

This is done by pressing the DRAW/DEAL button without having pressed any of the hold buttons.

You now press the DRAW/DEAL button to receive some new cards. The "HELD" cards will remain and those cards not chosen to be held will be replaced with new ones. This set of cards is the final hand.

If your hand is a winner, the machine will flash "**WINNER**" at the bottom of the screen. Winning hands are automatically paid according to the payoffs shown on the machine.

CREDIT

There is a useful feature offered on many video poker machines that allows you to play on winnings using a credit function built-in to the machines.

Let's say for example, that you've just hit a win for 20 coins. Two things will happen.

On the machine, you'll see "Credit - 20" appear. To continue playing without cashing out and reinserting coins, you can now press another button that will have lit up and be indicated by the label, **Maximum Bet**, **Bet 5** or some similar name. This allows you to play five of your 20 credits toward a new hand which will appear on the screen along with the information that your credit now stands at 15.

The second thing that will happen after your 20 coin win is that a button called the **Cashout** or **Payout** button will light up. If pressed, the machine will give immediate payment of the winnings registered in the credit area.

The Cashout button can be used after any hand is completed to cash out wins that have accumulated. If you want to continue playing on credit, keep pressing the Maximum Bet button to get a new hand dealt.

Let's go over the winning hands in video poker and then we'll show the payoffs you'll most likely encounter in the different games available.

The hands in the chart below are listed in ascending order, from weakest to strongest, as they are in the payoff charts in this section, with the exception of the Five of a Kind hand, which is usually stronger than a Royal Flush composed of wild cards but weaker than the Royal made naturally - without wild cards.

Winning Video Poker Hands

Jacks or Better - Two cards of equal value are called a pair. Jacks or better refers to a pair of Jacks, Queens, Kings or Aces.

Two Pair - Two sets of paired cards, such as 3-3 and 10-10.

Three of a Kind - Three cards of equal value, such as 9-9-9.

Straight - Five cards in numerical sequence, such as 3-4-5-6-7 or 10-J-Q-K-A. The ace can be counted as the highest card or the lowest card in a straight, however, it may not be in the middle of a five card run, such as Q-K-A-2-3, which is not a straight.

Flush - Any five cards of the same suit, such as five hearts.

Full House - Three of a kind and a pair, such as 2-2-2-J-J.

Four of a Kind - Four cards of equal value, such as K-K-K-K.

Straight Flush - A straight all in the same suit, such as 7-8-9-10-J, all in spades.

Royal Flush - 10-J-Q-K-A, all in the same suit.

Five of a Kind - Five cards of equal value, a hand that's only possible in wild card video poker. For example, if deuces are wild, the hand 2-2-7-7-7 would be five sevens.

Jacks or Better: 9-6 Machines

These machines are known as **9-6 machines**, because of the 9 and 6 coin payouts when the Full House and Flush are hit. Note that a pair of 10s will not pay anything back, nor will any lower pair. A hand of jacks or better is needed for a payout.

Payoffs on Jacks or Better • 9-6 Machine

Coins Played	1	2	3	4	5
Jacks or Better	1	2	3	4	5
Two Pair	2	4	6	8	10
Three of a Kind	3	6	9	12	15
Straight	4	8	12	16	20
Flush	6	12	18	24	30
Full House	9	18	27	36	45
Four of a Kind	25	50	75	100	125
Straight Flush	50	100	150	200	250
Royal Flush	250	500	750	1000	4000

Progressive Payout

Besides the straight machines discussed above, there are Progressive machines, as in slots.

All payoffs, like the straight machines are fixed except in the case of a Royal Flush, where this grandaddy pays the accumulated total posted above the machine on the electronic board. This total slowly, but constantly rises, and on a quarter machine in Las Vegas can rise into the thousands of dollars.

The following chart shows typical payoffs for video poker on a Jacks or Better Progressive machine. This machine is known as an **8-5 machine**, so named for the payoffs given on the full house and flush respectively.

Payoffs on Jacks or Better 8-5 Progressives

Coins Played	1	2	3	4	5
Jacks or Better	1	2	3	4	5
Two Pair	2	4	6	8	10
Three of a Kind	3	6	9	12	15
Straight	4	8	12	16	20
Flush	5	10	15	20	25
Full House	8	16	24	32	40
Four of a Kind	25	50	75	100	125
Straight Flush	50	100	150	200	250
Royal Flush	250	500	750	1000	*

*When five coins are played and the royal flush is hit, the bettor receives the full amount accumulated for the Progressive jackpot. Note that all five coins must be played to win the jackpot.

10s or Better Video Poker

The 10s or Better machine is only found infrequently. The following is the payout on the non-progressive machines. Note that Royal Flushes pay 800-1 only if five coins have been played.

Payoffs on 10s or Better

Coins Played	1	2	3	4	5
10s or Better	1	2	3	4	5
Two Pair	2	4	6	8	10
Three of a Kind	3	6	9	12	15
Straight	4	8	12	16	20
Flush	5	10	15	20	25
Full House	6	12	18	24	30
Four of a Kind	25	50	75	100	125
Straight Flush	50	100	150	200	250
Royal Flush	250	500	750	1000	4000

Wild Card Video Poker

Two variations of video poker that have caught on and gained in popularity are the **Deuces Wild** and **Jokers Wild** machines. Wild cards can be given any value or suit and the machine will interpret wild cards in the most advantageous way for the player.

For example, the hand 2 2 5 6 8 in Deuces Wild would be a straight, for one 2 can be used as a 7 and the other as either a 9 or 4. The deuces could also be used as eights to give three of a kind, but since the straight is more valuable to the player the machine will see it as a straight.

Wild card machines have different payoff schedules than the Jacks or Better machines, and these machines will start giving credit only on a three of a kind hand or better.

Deuces Wild Video Poker

This variation of video poker is played the same way as the Jacks or Better or 10s or Better machines and uses the same standard 52 card deck, but in this version there is one important difference - the four deuces (2s) are wild, and can be used as any card in the deck, even to make a five of a kind hand.

The video poker machine will recognize the best hand possible using the deuces and will automatically give credit for the maximum hand value that can be made.

Deuces Wild Video Poker Payout					
Coins Played	1	2	3	4	5
Three of a Kind	1	2	3	4	5
Straight	2	4	6	8	10
Flush	2	4	6	8	10
Full House	3	6	9	12	15
Four of a Kind	5	10	15	20	25
Straight Flush	9	18	27	36	45
Five of a Kind	15	30	45	60	75
Royal Flush (deuces)	25	50	75	100	125
Four Deuces	200	400	600	800	1000
Royal Flush (Natural)	250	500	750	1000	4000

Note that the Royal Flush as a natural hand (without the deuces) will be paid off at 800-1 only if five coins are played.

Joker Wild Video Poker

There are two version of the Joker Wild game: **Ace-King** and **Two Pairs**. In the Ace-King version, a minimum hand of a pair of kings must be made for a payoff. In Two Pairs, two pair is the minimum hand needed for a payoff.

Both versions of Joker Wild are played with a 53 card deck, the regular 52 card deck plus the wild card, the **joker**, which can be assigned any value.

Let's look at the payoffs for each Joker Wild game in turn.

Keep in mind that the Royal Flush will only be paid off with the maximum return if five coins are played.

Joker Wild Video Poker Payout • Ace-King					
Coins Played	1	2	3	4	5
Ace or Kings	1	2	3	4	5
Two Pair	1	2	3	4	5
Three of a Kind	2	4	6	8	10
Straight	3	6	9	12	15
Flush	5	10	15	20	25
Full House	7	14	21	28	35
Four of a Kind	20	40	60	80	100
Straight Flush	50	100	150	200	250
Royal Flush (Joker)	100	200	300	400	500
Five of a Kind	200	400	600	800	1000
Royal Flush (natural)	250	500	750	1000	4000

Note the same payout whether one gets a pair of Aces or Kings, or Two Pair.

Sometimes a machine will be found that pays off only 15 for 1 on the four of a kind instead of the 20 for 1 as listed above. Give these machines a miss.

Joker Wild Video Poker Payout • Two Pair				
Coins Played	**1**	**2**	**3**	**4**	**5**
Two Pair	1	2	3	4	5
Three of a Kind	2	4	6	8	10
Straight	5	10	15	20	25
Flush	7	14	21	28	35
Full House	8	16	24	32	40
Four of a Kind	20	40	60	80	100
Straight Flush	50	100	150	200	250
Royal Flush (Joker)	50	100	150	200	250
Five of a Kind	100	200	300	400	500
Royal Flush (natural)	250	500	750	1000	4000

Note that five coins must be played, and should always be played, to receive the maximum payout for the Royal Flush. For example, the Royal Flush will pay out 4,000 coins or $1,000, for a quarter machine when five coins are played, while four coins would yield only 1/4 as much - $250.

Getting a Straight Flush with five coins will pay 250 coins or $62.50 and a Full House will pay 45 coins or $11.25 for that same quarter machine.

WINNING STRATEGIES

The big payoff on video poker machines is for the royal flush. It doesn't matter what variation is played - Jacks or Better, 10s or Better, Deuces Wild or Joker Wild - a whopping 4,000 coins are paid for this big daddy when five coins are played.

And on progressive machines, if a full five coins are played, the total could be a great deal higher, making the game even more interesting for the player trying to land himself or herself a jackpot to remember.

Of course, the royal doesn't come often. With correct strategy, you'll hit one every 30,000+ hands on the average. This doesn't mean, however, that you won't hit one in your very first hour of play!

But meanwhile, you'll be collecting other winners such as straights, full houses and the like, and with proper play, all in all, you can beat the video poker machines. To win, you must play the correct strategies. Like regular poker, there are skillful ways to play your hand.

However, unlike regular poker, you're not playing against other players, but against a machine, and the strategies must be adjusted accordingly. Strategies that make sense in the Friday night game may not be the proper ones at a video poker machine.

Always Play Five Coins

To achieve the absolute best odds at the video poker machine, five coins must be played. At first glance, this suggestion probably strikes you as being strange. Why not one coin or two? After all, the payoffs on all hands at the video poker machine are proportionately the same whether one, two, three, four or five coins are played.

However, there's one glaring exception - the royal flush.

And though this hand doesn't come often, it does come and much more so than in a regular poker game for we're playing an entirely different strategy in video poker. We're concentrating on the big score, the royal flush, as opposed to a regular poker game, where your primary goal is simply to win the hand, even if a pair of sevens do the trick. And in video poker, a pair of sevens is worth nothing - the machine gives no payoff for it.

We're playing the odds at the machines, and you'll find yourself throwing away hands that you would never do in a regular poker game. But like we mentioned above, video poker is not a regular poker game.

Look back at the payoff chart for Jacks or Better and notice what happens on the royal flush payoffs.

Interesting, yes? One coin played returns 200 coins, two coins yields 400, three coins 600 and four coins brings home 800 bad boys. Well, the progression for the fifth coin should be 1,000 if you're following along with the addition. But it's not.

The full payoff on a royal flush with five coins played is 4,000 coins! Now that's a nice payoff and that's also the reason we're going to be playing five coins. The royal is not as remote as it seems. You may never see one in a regular poker game, but at the video poker machines, following the strategies we suggest, you have a good chance to stare one in the face as the ringing bells mesmerize your gambling psyche.

You'll see similar jumps for the Royal Flush payoffs on all the video poker machines.

Therefore, to collect the full payoff on a royal flush, proper play dictates that you always play the full five coins for each game. For if you do hit the royal flush, there's a big, big difference between 1,000 coins returned and 4,000 returned.

Of course, less serious players can play any amount of coins from 1 to 5 and still enjoy the game.

Find Machines With the Best Payoffs

The payoff schedules we've listed in this section are not the only ones you'll find for the games we've discussed.

You may find machines with less generous payouts, so as a general rule, and when possible, always choose machines with better payouts.

For example, when there's a lot of casino competition, such as Las Vegas, a little window shopping will definitely be to your advantage.

Winning Strategy for Jacks or Better:

Following is the basic strategy for the 9-6 machines. (These strategies are not applicable to the 8-5 Jacks or Better Progressives.)*

1. Whenever you hold <u>four cards to a royal flush</u>, discard the fifth card, even if that card gives you a flush or pair.
2. Keep a <u>jacks or better pair</u> and any higher hand such as a three of a kind or straight over three to the royal. Play the <u>three to a royal</u> over any lesser hand such as a low pair or four flush.
3. With <u>two cards to a royal</u>, keep four straights, four flushes, and high pairs or better instead. Otherwise, go for the royal.
4. Never break up a <u>straight or flush</u>, unless a one card draw gives you a chance for the royal.

*The full strategy charts for the 9-6 machines and the strategy charts for the 8-5 Progressives are beyond the scope of this book. Serious players looking to have the mathematical advantage and win money at video poker must buy GRI's Professional Video Poker Strategy listed in the back.

5. Keep <u>jacks or better</u> over a four straight or four flush.

6. Never break up a <u>four of a kind</u>, <u>full house</u>, <u>three of a kind</u> and <u>two pair</u> hands. The *rags*, worthless cards for the latter two hands, should be dropped on the draw.

7. The <u>jacks or better pair</u> is always kept, except when you have four cards to the royal, or four to the straight flush.

8. Keep <u>low pairs</u> over the four straight, but discard them in favor of the four flushes and three or four to a royal flush.

9. When dealt <u>unmade hands</u>, a pre-draw hands with no payable combination of cards, save in order, four to a royal flush and straight flush, three to a royal flush, four flushes, four straights, three to a straight flush, two cards to the royal, two cards jack or higher and one card jack or higher.

10. Lacking any of the above, with no card jack or higher, discard all the cards and draw five fresh ones.

Simplified Basic Strategy Chart

The following chart sums up the simplified basic strategy for Jacks or Better. The hands are listed in order of strength from most powerful first, the Royal Flush, to the least powerful last, the garbage hands.

Keep the hands listed higher in preference to hands listed lower. For example, you'll keep a High Pair over a three to a royal, but throw it away in favor of a four to the royal.

Jacks or Better
Simplified Basic Strategy Chart

Hand to Be Held	Cards Held	Cards Drawn
Royal Flush	5	0
Straight Flush	5	0
Four of a Kind	5	0
Full House	5	0
Four to a Royal	4	1
Flush	5	0
Three of a Kind	3	2
Straight	5	0
Four to a Straight Flush	4	1
Two Pair	4	1
High Pair	2	3
Three to a Royal	3	2
Four to a Flush	4	1
Low Pair	2	3
Four to a Straight	4	1
Three to a Straight Flush	3	2
Two to a Royal	2	3
Two High Cards	2	3
One High Card	1	4
Garbage Hand - Draw Five	0	5

Winning Strategy for 10s or Better

10s or Better is played similarly to Jacks or Better, except that you should keep a pair of 10s instead of discarding them for they yield a payoff.

Otherwise, follow the strategy as outlined above in Jacks or Better Winning Strategy.

Winning Strategy for Deuces Wild

Deuces are extremely valuable cards so when you get them, make sure you never discard them by accident. You'll notice that there is no payoff for hands less than three of a kind, so our strategy must be adjusted accordingly.

The key in Deuces Wild as in the non-wild versions is to go for the big payouts - the royal flush. Therefore, when you have three cards toward a royal flush discard the other two and go for it. Of course, the same holds true when you have four to the royal. Thus, if you have two deuces and a 10 or higher, along with two sub-10 cards of no value, go for the royal.

Similarly, if you have two deuces and three cards below the 10 in value, dump the crap and hang onto the deuces, unless two of the cards are paired in which case you have four of a kind, or the two cards retained give you four cards toward a straight flush.

If you hold one or two deuces with nothing else that's interesting, dump the junk and hang onto the deuces. If you're hand is really poor, and you're dealt five unrelated cards, get rid of them all and go for five fresh ones.

Three card flushes or straights are worthless in this game as are single unmatched high cards so don't be holding onto hands of this nature. You'll also get rid of two pair hands - for they don't pay. Hang onto one of the pairs, and go for three new cards.

If one of the pairs is teamed with a wild deuce, keep the three of a kind. However, if the deuce forms a high pair, it does no good at all and as suggested above, keep the deuce and draw four new cards.

Keep a pair at the outset, unless you've got a three card straight flush or royal flush going, in which case you'll dump the pair and go for the gold.

You'll find that many of the hands you'll be dealt will contain nothing worth saving and you'll be drawing for five fresh cards. Three card straights and flushes fit in this category along with some of the others we've mentioned. In any case, don't be afraid to discard your original five cards if they hold nothing of value.

It will take a little while getting used to wild card video poker after playing the non-wild versions, but once you get accustomed you should have a lot of fun at these machines.

Summary of Winning Strategy

Video poker is certainly a fun game, for it is a game of skill, and as we stated in the beginning, with proper play you can have the edge over the casino.

Like blackjack, you need to study the correct strategies carefully to come out a winner.

For those players serious about winning money at video poker, the professional video poker strategy advertised in the back is highly recommended. You'll learn the important differences in strategy between the 8-5 Progressive and 9-6 Jacks or Better machines, and receive complete strategy charts for these games, the wild card games, and others.

Meanwhile, use your skill to good advantage, and see if you can't beat the house and be a winner!

Baccarat Master Card Counter
NEW WINNING STRATEGY!

For the **first time**, Gambling Research Institute releases the **latest winning techniques** at baccarat. This **exciting** strategy, played by big money players in Monte Carlo and other exclusive locations, is based on principles that have made insiders and pros **hundreds of thousands of dollars** counting cards at blackjack - card counting!

NEW WINNING APPROACH

This brand **new** strategy now applies card counting to baccarat to give you a **new winning approach,** and is designed so that any player, with just a little effort, can successfully take on the casinos at their own game - and win!

SIMPLE TO USE, EASY TO MASTER

You learn how to count cards for baccarat without the mental effort needed for blackjack! No need to memorize numbers - keep the count on the scorepad. Easy-to-use, play the strategy while enjoying the game!

LEARN WHEN TO BET BANKER, WHEN TO BET PLAYER

No longer will you make bets on hunches and guesses - use the GRI Baccarat Master Card Counter to determine when to bet Player and when to bet Banker. You learn the basic counts (running and true), deck favorability, when to increase bets and much more in this **winning strategy**.

LEARN TO WIN IN JUST ONE SITTING

That's right! After **just one sitting** you'll be able to successfully learn this powerhouse strategy and use it to your advantage at the baccarat table. Be the best baccarat player at the table - the one playing the odds to **win**! Baccarat can be beaten. The Master Card Counter shows you how!

FREE BONUS!

Order now to receive **absolutely free**, The Basics of Winning Baccarat. One quick reading with this great primer shows you how to play and win.

To order, send $50 by bank check or money order to:

Cardoza Publishing.P.O. Box 1500, Cooper Station, New York, NY 10276

Handheld Video Poker

Handheld Draw Poker

Handheld Pro Blackjack

PROFESSIONAL VIDEO POKER STRATEGY
Win at Video Poker - With the Odds!

At last, for the **first time**, and for **serious players only**, the GRI **Professional Video Poker** strategy is released so you too can play to win! **You read it right** - this strategy gives you the **mathematical advantage** over the casino and what's more, it's **easy to learn!**

PROFESSIONAL STRATEGY SHOWS YOU HOW TO WIN WITH THE ODDS

This **powerhouse strategy**, played for **big profits** by an **exclusive** circle of **professionals**, people who make their living at the machines, is now made available to you! You too can win - with the odds - and this **winning strategy** shows you how!

HOW TO PLAY FOR A PROFIT

You'll learn the **key factors** to play on a **pro level**: which machines will turn you a profit, break-even and win rates, hands per hour and average win per hour charts, time value, team play and more! You'll also learn big play strategy, alternate jackpot play, high and low jackpot play and key strategies to follow.

WINNING STRATEGIES FOR ALL MACHINES

This **comprehensive, advanced pro package** not only shows you how to win money at the 8-5 progressives, but also, the **winning strategies** for 10s or better, deuces wild, joker's wild, flat-top, progressive and special options features.

BE A WINNER IN JUST ONE DAY

In just one day, after learning our strategy, you will have the skills to **consistently win money** at video poker - with the odds. The strategies are easy to use under practical casino conditions.

BONUS - PROFESSIONAL PROFIT EXPECTANCY FORMULA ($15 VALUE)

For serious players, we're including this bonus essay which discusses the profit expectancy principles of video poker and how to relate them to real dollars and cents in your game.

To order, send $50 by check or money order to <u>Cardoza Publishing</u>

GRI s Professional Video Poker Strategy - Just $50

Yes! Please *rush* me GRI's Professional Video Poker Strategy and the free bonus ($15 value), Professional Profit Expectancey Formula. Enclosed is a check or money order for $50 (plus postage and handling) made out to:

Cardoza Publishing
P.O. Box 1500, Cooper Station, New York, NY 10276
MC/VISA/AMEX orders by phone (718)743-5229

Include $3.50 postage and handling for U.S. & Canada, other countries $7.00. Orders outside U.S., money order payable in U.S. dollars on U.S. bank only.

NAME _____

ADDRESS _____

CITY _____ STATE _____ ZIP _____

Offer valid only with coupon - 30 Day Money Back Guarantee! CAS PL

156

158